THE FUTURE FIT ORGANISATION

A LEADER'S GUIDE TO TRANSFORMATION

Friska Wirya

'I highly recommend this book to executives struggling to shift the needle forward on their transformation – those who need to disrupt without being disruptive.'

I Yip, Founder and CEO Avertro (ex CTO McAfee APAC)

'In *The Future Fit Organisation*, Friska Wirya makes a clear case for change – not just in technology but more importantly, in the right "people stack", infused with innovation and creativity. I highly recommend her manifesto as entertainingly readable and eminently actionable!'

C Van Den Hende, VP Digital Transformation, Mars and author *Goodbye, Orchid*

'Leading transformation is a critical part of the modern C-suite job: we all need an understanding of the people stack – this is an eye-opening and industry-changing how-to guide for all executives.'

S Spiteri, CEO and NED (ex Google, News Corp, *The Economist*)

'*The Future Fit Organisation* is a blueprint for leaders who want to realise the full benefits of their digital transformation. A must-read for the leaders of today.'

D Mcburnie, Founder and CEO Versor, former Head of Data & AI APAC, Chief Digital Officer Fujitsu

'This book highlights importantly that in achieving unconventional results, you will need to alter your thinking approach. The neglected yet essential process of "unlearning" beliefs and behaviour is both a critical life and business skill in today's world.'

B Andrews, President Worley

'An indispensable guide to winning heads, hearts and minds during transformation. A relevant and timely book for leaders who must transform their businesses.'

J Ch'Ng, Founder and Chairman, B2BE

'This is an invaluable guidebook on how leaders can create the conditions for innovation and growth to occur – regardless of industry or geography.'

J Dalitz, NED at Qudos Bank, iPartners, Australian Museum

'This is a book I'll be turning to time and time again to guide and evolve my strategies to transform with minimal pain.'

B Lawson, Chair, Djakarta Mining Club

'Friska highlights the importance of mindset as a driving factor in creating and nurturing a fit organisation. Openness to learning and change are critical elements of any successful company and team, and Friska provides specific and detailed examples from which even the most seasoned CEO and leadership can learn. Throughout the pages of her book, Friska reminds us to keep asking the questions that will enable us to create an organisational environment that can effectively adjust and thrive.'

Joe Hyrkin, CEO Issuu

CONTENTS

INTRODUCTION

I can't help but laugh. It's funny how someone who has made change her calling card (i.e. me!) stumbled upon the change management discipline out of sheer curiosity.

I get bored easily; and boy was I bored in general management consulting. Back then, in the early 2010s, change management was still new. It intrigued me. It was hard to describe: a discipline that was coming of age. It played to my strengths. Every day was different. So was every culture, every organisation and every project.

I took a gamble and backed myself, taking a 40 per cent pay cut to cut my teeth as a change analyst. I worked my way up with unwavering dedication and laser-like focus.

I've been exposed to all sorts of changes: physiological change; technological change; culture change; structural change; strategy change; leadership change; process and systemic change. I've worked on great projects: assuring the safety and quality of life of 1.2 million people by establishing the future of policing for Western Australia, the world's largest single policing jurisdiction; establishing an offshoring program, by standing up delivery centres in Hyderabad, Mumbai and Chennai to lift communities out of poverty, and enable developed countries to step up and do value-adding work.

I've worked on some really difficult projects, too, which eroded my mental health in a big way. The days seemed like months, with resentment, aggression, sabotage and bullying rife among the client organisation. No-one likes change, yet it's my job to make it happen. Quickly and safely.

Seven years after my first change analyst role I was a newly crowned Head of Change for the biggest gold miner in the Southern Hemisphere. I then helped the University of Melbourne – Australia's answer to Harvard – execute its COVID-19 response, pivoting to a fully remote campus as the pandemic took hold and Melbourne endured the lengthiest and strictest lockdowns in the world.

Since then, I have cherrypicked a select number of clients to partner with, supporting them to bring organisational changes they had only dreamed about into reality. I also impart my knowledge of change to thousands in the form of keynotes, masterclasses and webinars.

As a global top 50 change management thought leader (Thinkers360), I have spent years working with organisations to help them adapt and thrive in an ever-changing world. However, as we move further into the 21st century, it's becoming increasingly clear that the rules of the game are changing faster than ever before. Organisations must be agile, innovative and able to pivot quickly to keep up with the pace of change.

Don't take my word for it; here are some scary stats.

According to research by McKinsey Global Institute, the pace of technological change is ten times faster and at 300 times the scale, or roughly 3000 times the impact, of the Industrial Revolution.[1]

The average lifespan of a company listed on the S&P 500 has decreased from 67 years in the 1920s to just 15 years today, according to a study by Innosight.[2]

In 2020 the COVID-19 pandemic accelerated the adoption of remote work, with a Gartner survey stating 88 per cent of organisations worldwide encouraged or required employees to work from home.[3]

The pace of new product development has accelerated over time. For example, the development of the Boeing 707 aircraft took four years, while the development of the Boeing 787 – a much larger and more complicated vehicle – took only three years, according to a report by PwC.[4]

The pace of change in the financial industry is also accelerating with the rise of fintech companies and the adoption of blockchain technology. Accenture found global investment in fintech increased from $928 million in 2008 to $27.4 billion in 2017.[5]

These statistics highlight the increasing speed and scale of change across a range of industries and sectors. As a result, organisations must be able to adapt quickly and effectively to remain competitive in a rapidly evolving business environment.

This is where the concept of future fitness comes in. Much like physical fitness, future fitness is about building the resilience, strength and flexibility that organisations need to survive in the years to come.

Despite the urgent need for organisations to become future fit, the failure rate of change initiatives and digital transformations remains alarmingly high. We've all heard the research suggesting up to 70 per cent of change initiatives fail to achieve their intended goals, and the failure rate for digital transformation projects is even higher.[6]

Unfortunately, this trend has not improved; and it is unlikely to any time soon. As everything in our world – social norms, technology, culture, politics, legislation and environment – continues to evolve at an unprecedented pace, organisations must grapple with increasingly complex and rapidly changing systems. At the same time, employees and customers are demanding more from the organisations they interact with, placing greater pressure on leaders to change not just for change's sake – but to innovate, evolve and grow.

In this context, the need for future fitness has never been more urgent.

This book aims to equip leaders and organisations with the tools, strategies and mindset they need to thrive in the face of ongoing change and disruption.

I will explore change management research, organisational psychology and contemporary leadership, providing practical advice drawing on more than a decade of experience helping the world's largest organisations become future fit. I've also included reflection questions at the end of each chapter, designed to broaden your thinking and provide a starting point for self-assessment and exploration.

This book is a blueprint of principles, tools and techniques that are relevant no matter what industry you're in or where you're located. My hope is that you walk away from this book with the confidence to create a future fit organisation that is ready to tackle the challenges of tomorrow.

CHAPTER 1

REDEFINING LITERACY FOR THE FUTURE

Let me ask you some questions: are you future fit? Is your organisation future fit? What does future fitness *even mean* to you? Does your mind conjure up images of barbells and bench presses?

Future fitness has nothing to do with muscles. Renowned futurist Alvin Toffler said, 'The illiterate of the 21st century will not be those who cannot read or write, but those who cannot learn, relearn, and unlearn.'

Like Toffler, I argue that future literacy is determined by your ability to continuously learn and unlearn.

Future means 'at a later time'; and fitness can be described as the quality of being suitable to fulfil a particular role or task. Combining the two, future fitness is being capable, fit and

healthy so you can leverage what is yet to come. It's to be resilient, nimble and agile, to roll with the punches, to be dynamic, to go with the flow like water (thanks, Bruce Lee). To be future fit, you need a fluid, flexible mind that seeks out change over comfort.

The rapid pace of technological advancement means that the skills and knowledge that were relevant just a few years ago may no longer be applicable in today's world. The material you learn today at university may be obsolete by the time you graduate. In the past decade, we have seen the rise of artificial intelligence (AI), blockchain technology and the Internet of Things (IoT). These developments have led to the creation of new industries and job roles that did not exist before. AI has led to autonomous vehicles, chatbots and virtual assistants, as well as roles such as data scientist, machine learning engineer and AI ethicist.

Blockchain birthed the cryptocurrency and smart contracts industries, and roles such as blockchain developer, architect and analyst. The IoT triggered a mushrooming of smart homes, smart cities and connected healthcare, with roles such as IoT architect, IoT security specialist and IoT data analyst now commonplace.

Individuals and organisations must adapt quickly and continuously learn new skills to remain relevant. Being future fit also requires mental agility and flexibility. As humans, we have a natural tendency to resist change and cling to what we know. We find comfort and safety in the familiar. This approach is unsustainable – it will not help us get to where we want to be tomorrow. We must be open to new ideas, perspectives and ways of working, and be willing to unlearn old habits and beliefs that are no longer serving us. All of us, to some extent, walk around

INDIVIDUALS AND ORGANISATIONS MUST ADAPT QUICKLY AND CONTINUOUSLY LEARN NEW SKILLS TO REMAIN RELEVANT.

burdened by unhelpful, sometimes destructive behaviours. Multiply that by however many employees an organisation has, and you can see why this bad-behaviour baggage will impede our ability to stay ahead of the curve.

Being future fit also means embracing diversity and inclusivity. The world is becoming more connected and globalised, and organisations must be able to work effectively with people from diverse backgrounds and cultures. This requires not only tolerance but also a genuine appreciation and understanding of different perspectives.

Future fitness is not about physical fitness or even specific technical skills. Rather, it concerns mental agility, adaptability and openness to change. It requires us to embrace uncertainty and be willing to make a few tumbles when we're trying something new. Those who are future fit will be well positioned to succeed in the years to come, while those who resist change will find themselves left behind.

Comfort zones are dangerous things. We must realise that when we step beyond our comfort zone we're not entering our *discomfort* zone, but rather our zone of growth, progress and innovation.

> **THE WORLD HATES CHANGE. YET IT IS THE ONLY THING THAT HAS BROUGHT PROGRESS.**
>
> CHARLES KETTERING

No change, no progress

Change is the catalyst for progress, and progress is what propels society forward. All significant advancements in human history have come about through change. The discovery of penicillin, for example, revolutionised medicine, and the use of electricity has transformed our world. The iPhone, Airbnb and Uber are some examples of disruptive innovations that have fundamentally altered the way we communicate and travel.

But change can be uncomfortable, and it can be difficult to let go of the old ways of doing things. Some managers, for instance, still measure their employees' value based on the number of hours they spend in the office, rather than the outcomes they achieve. These outdated approaches hinder progress and innovation. No-one likes a clock watcher. Unfortunately, many managers in today's organisations still regard desk time as contribution.

The COVID-19 pandemic accelerated the need for change, as governments, businesses and individuals alike had to quickly adapt to new ways of working, living, learning and parenting. Managers who were used to measuring productivity based on physical presence in the office were forced to re-evaluate their approach when remote work became the norm. This shift in mindset saw a boom in outcome-driven measures when assessing job performance, where physical presence was no longer mandatory. This change was felt across the world, from Mumbai to Manila to Melbourne.

ALL PROGRESS INVOLVES CHANGE, BUT NOT ALL CHANGE RESULTS IN PROGRESS.

All progress involves change, but not all change results in progress. Keep reading to make sure the changes you instigate fall in the former category.

Future fitness = digital transformation

True digital transformation is rare. Most organisations are undergoing a glacial evolution, at best.

4

For me, digital transformation is the combination of digital adoption and proficiency, effective change leadership and a structured approach to elicit enterprise-wide behaviour change.

Digital transformation is essential for organisations to become future fit. True digital transformation is not just about using new technology tools; it is a fundamental change in the way a company operates and creates value. Transformation requires solid change leaders: individuals who can lead by example and inspire others to embrace a new way of working. It involves adopting new technologies and, more importantly, ensuring proficiency in their use. Companies need to reimagine their operating model and role in the value chain to stay ahead of the curve.

> # THE ENTERPRISE THAT DOES NOT INNOVATE AGES AND DECLINES, AND IN A PERIOD OF RAPID CHANGE SUCH AS THE PRESENT, THE DECLINE WILL BE FAST.
>
> ## PETER DRUCKER

The COVID-19 pandemic was a catalyst for most organisations to embrace digital transformation. Many had to adapt quickly and invest in virtual collaboration tools such as Teams, Miro, Webex or Google Meet. Automation of low-value processes has also become a priority for many organisations to increase efficiency and reduce costs. AI is increasingly being used to predict demand levels and automate decision-making processes. Organisations such as Amazon, Walmart, Coca-Cola and Alibaba have implemented automation technologies to optimise inventory management, tighten supply chains, reduce waste and improve delivery scheduling. Banks such as Emirates NBD and DBS Bank are using AI to project demand for products, automate credit approval processes and improve efficiency in back-office and risk-management processes. While some may view these strategies as low-level, most of these technologies were not even on the business radar a few years ago. Zoom was something you did around a race-track, not a platform you dialled into.

Digital transformation is not just about implementing new technologies, though; it's about creating a culture of innovation where experimentation and learning are encouraged. It requires the willingness to take risks and fail fast to drive regular improvements in performance. Companies that are future fit are not afraid to challenge the status quo and embrace new ways of thinking and doing. They continuously seek opportunities to level up and remain agile in the face of change. Digital transformation is not a one-time event; it is an ongoing process that requires continuous learning and adaptation. By embracing digital transformation, companies can remain relevant and competitive in an increasingly digital world.

> **CLEARLY, THE THING THAT'S TRANSFORMING IS NOT THE TECHNOLOGY – THE TECHNOLOGY IS TRANSFORMING YOU.**
>
> **JEANNE W ROSS**

So ask yourself: is your organisation really transforming, or simply evolving?

Organisational unlearning and relearning

The COVID-19 pandemic forced organisations and individuals to adapt and change the way they operate. However, many of the changes implemented were temporary and don't represent a true transformation.

To truly succeed in the post-pandemic world, we all need to be willing to relearn and unlearn. Relearning involves acquiring the new skills and knowledge necessary for navigating constantly changing circumstances. Many organisations had to quickly pivot to remote work during the pandemic, requiring employees to learn new technologies and work processes. However, relearning goes beyond just acquiring new skills – it also involves being willing to let go of old habits and ways of doing things that are no longer effective.

Unlearning involves reprogramming old beliefs and assumptions that no longer hold true. This is more challenging than relearning because it requires individuals and organisations to confront deeply ingrained beliefs and put their thought processes and beliefs under the microscope. For example, many organisations still hold onto the belief that in-person meetings and work are necessary for productivity, despite evidence to the contrary.[7] To truly transform and become future fit, organisations must be willing to both relearn and unlearn, and dive into experimentation, failure, reflection and iteration until the right solutions are found.

The pandemic had a silver lining: changes that were previously deemed impossible, taking several years and a cast of thousands to achieve, were suddenly made a reality – seemingly overnight – when the onset of the virus sent shockwaves around the world. We had to change the way we worked, the way we parented, the way we led and the way we created value. There were many hero stories of reinvention and adaptability, both within large global companies and microbusinesses. Gin distilleries transformed into hand sanitiser manufacturers; clothing designers started making masks. In Melbourne, the most locked-down city in the world, a make-up artist who specialised in working with Chinese brides was in despair with her entire income wiped out. She thought about how she could pivot and reinvent. She turned to YouTube and began offering free make-up

tutorials. The popularity of her instructional videos translated into paid one-on-one make-up lessons conducted over Zoom. Her reputation steadily grew as each lockdown progressed, and she now rakes in more through advertising revenue than make-up applications.

One of the world's top restaurants, fine dining establishment Attica pivoted from degustation to delivery. Located in the leafy unassuming suburb of Ripponlea, it offered a $65 menu of classic dishes and family favourites such as lasagne and chocolate cake for delivery during lockdown. It was a far cry from its $395 per head dining-in option.

> **THE GREATEST DANGER IN TIMES OF TURBULENCE IS NOT THE TURBULENCE – IT IS TO ACT WITH YESTERDAY'S LOGIC.**
>
> **UNKNOWN**

While its shops were shuttered around the world, Louis Vuitton stayed close to its customers. The brand leveraged communication channels such as Weibo and WhatsApp to engage its exclusive clientele. The pandemic resulted in its most profitable year to date.

Even larger, harder-to-shift organisations have already embraced the future fit approach. Companies such as Amazon and Google are constantly experimenting with new technologies and processes, and are willing to fail in order to learn and improve. They have built cultures of continuous learning, enabling them to stay ahead of the curve in rapidly changing markets.

Change has been necessary in all industries. While many organisations adapted and transformed during the pandemic, some struggled to do so. Some traditional bricks-and-mortar retailers that were slow to embrace e-commerce and online sales suffered as more customers shifted to shopping online. JCPenney, a major department store chain in the US, filed for bankruptcy in 2020 after years of declining sales and struggling to compete with online retailers such as Amazon.

Some industries that rely heavily on in-person interactions and events were hit hard. The travel and hospitality industry faced significant challenges as people cancelled travel plans and avoided crowded public spaces. Airlines and hotels were forced to lay off employees and implement cost-cutting measures to stay afloat. Once the 'COVID-normal' period began they faced a different challenge: needing to rehire and retrain staff as restrictions were lifted and overseas travel restarted with gusto.

Another example is the education sector. Many institutions struggled to adapt to online learning and provide high-quality remote education. Some universities faced criticism for charging high tuition fees for virtual classes that were not seen to be as effective as in-person instruction. However, other institutions have successfully transitioned to online learning and found new opportunities for growth in the digital space. Harvard University has been offering online courses for over a decade through its Harvard Extension School and HarvardX programs. The university partnered with edX, a nonprofit online learning platform, to offer massive open online courses (MOOCs) to learners around the world. Coursera has continued to expand, partnering with other organisations to offer courses, certificates and degree programs to more than 77 million registered learners. Believe it or not, the University of Phoenix has been offering online degree programs since 1989! The university has more than 100,000 online learners and has been recognised for its flexible and innovative approach to higher education.

Overall, the pandemic highlighted the importance of adaptability and the need for organisations to be able to pivot quickly in response to unexpected challenges. Those able to do so emerged stronger and more resilient, while those that were unable to adapt struggled to survive.

THE ENLIGHTENED LEADERS WHO SEE CHANGE AS AN OPPORTUNITY, INSTEAD OF AN OBSTACLE, WILL HAVE THE FIRST-MOVER ADVANTAGE.

In contrast, organisations that are resistant to change and unwilling to adapt will be left behind and irrelevant. Change is the next normal. The enlightened leaders who see change as an opportunity, instead of an obstacle, will have the first-mover advantage, affording them additional precious time to experiment, explore and iterate with new ideas and innovations.

No-one wants to be the next taxi that is Ubered into oblivion. Few actually do something about it. Which camp do you fall into?

PAUSE AND REFLECT

- What does 'future fit' mean to you and your organisation? Reflect on the key characteristics and capabilities that you believe will be essential for success in an ever-evolving business landscape.

- How prepared is your organisation for the challenges and disruptions that lie ahead? Consider your current strategies, structures and culture, and assess their alignment with the need for adaptability, innovation and resilience.

- What are the potential barriers and opportunities that arise when striving to become a future fit organisation? Reflect on the changes and transformations that may be required, as well as the potential resistance or support from stakeholders within and outside the organisation.

CHAPTER 2

THE PERILS OF POOR CHANGE MANAGEMENT

A 2021 Fortune study stated 85 per cent of companies are accelerating their transformations. That's a lot of change.[8]

Ironically, although change is the only constant, the 80 per cent failure rate of change initiatives hasn't budged for decades.[9] The original bleak statistic was 70 per cent, according to *Harvard Business Review*, with a more pessimistic statistic purported by Kaplan & Norton's Balanced Scorecard.[10]

Change failure is a pervasive problem that has been around for my entire career. The reality is, most companies attempting to change end up failing. It's a sobering thought.

The 2000 acquisition of Time Warner by America Online (AOL) for US$165 billion is one of the most high-profile examples of failed change management. The merger was hailed as a game changer for the media industry but ended up being one of the most expensive corporate disasters in history. The deal resulted in massive losses for shareholders and the resignation of key executives. The chairman attributed a lack of change management, leading to an irreversible clash of corporate cultures, as the reason for the failure. Toshiba's accounting scandal is another example of failed change. The company overstated profits by billions of dollars. Process, policy and required culture change to mitigate the scandal's impact and prevent it from recurring in future was not handled well, leading to the resignation of its CEO and a significant decline in its stock price.

Change initiative failure can also, of course, occur in smaller companies. Many businesses have implemented systems that are never used, with their investment in these systems becoming a complete waste of resources. This highlights the importance of effective change management and the need for companies to ensure that their investment in change yields a healthy return.

It's understandable that people may be sceptical of change announcements, given how often these initiatives fail. However, it's important for companies to recognise that change is necessary for survival in today's business landscape. Successful change implementation requires a solid change management strategy, change leaders who can role model and advocate for a different way of doing things, and the adoption of new tools and processes. Companies that can manage change effectively and embrace digital transformation will be those thriving today and well into the future.

SUCCESSFUL CHANGE IMPLEMENTATION REQUIRES A SOLID CHANGE MANAGEMENT STRATEGY, CHANGE LEADERS WHO CAN ROLE MODEL AND ADVOCATE FOR A DIFFERENT WAY OF DOING THINGS, AND THE ADOPTION OF NEW TOOLS AND PROCESSES.

Why do we keep failing to change?

In my experience, one of the biggest reasons for the high failure rate of change is that many organisations approach change in a haphazard manner: it's something that's done 'when there's a business critical project' or 'when there's leftover budget'. They may not have a clear plan in place or they may not communicate the changes effectively – if at all – to employees. There may be a lack of accountability for those leading the change, leading to a lack of direction and follow-through.

Another reason is the resistance to change that exists within many organisations. Resistance is normal; it protected us from unknown dangers in the prehistoric era. Change is often difficult and uncomfortable, and employees will naturally resist changes to their routines.

The problem is that organisations don't realise that resistance can be turned into resilience – with effort, intention, dedication and commitment. Instead of proactively engaging and managing resistance, most ignore it or try to beat people into submission. And without proper buy-in from employees and stakeholders, change initiatives falter.

I wonder what would have happened to Nokia if its leaders hadn't resisted or denied the realities of the burgeoning smartphone market? A lack of internal buy-in caused the company to exit the mobile phone business in 2014, with Microsoft swooping in to buy it out. Despite recognising the potential of the smartphone market, Nokia's executives were hesitant to invest in the new technology and believed their feature-phone business would continue to be successful. They failed to anticipate the speed and scale of the digital disruption, and didn't adapt quickly enough to changing consumer tastes and market conditions.

Change initiatives are often too focused on short-term results and fail to consider the long-term implications. When organisations prioritise short-term gains over long-term planning and strategy, they may fail to anticipate potential roadblocks or obstacles that could arise in the future. This is a major driver of culture change failure. CEOs are usually remunerated against a rising share price and quarterly results, not long-term metrics such as organisational health and employee wellbeing.

As I've said, the rapid pace of technological advancement and increasing complexity of the business world means that organisations must adapt quickly to stay competitive. However, this can also lead to a sense of overwhelming pressure and uncertainty, which can make it difficult for organisations to effectively plan and implement change initiatives in a clear, logical way.

CHANGE BEFORE YOU HAVE TO.

JACK WELCH

It is clear that change management is a complex and challenging process that requires careful planning, communication and execution. Unfortunately the majority of organisations don't give change the prioritisation, investment and attention it needs – hence the stubbornly high failure rate.

Change is harder today

You're not imagining it; change *is* getting harder to land.

In today's fast-paced and hyperconnected world, change management has become increasingly difficult. The perfect storm has been brewing, with various factors making it harder to implement successful change initiatives. One of the biggest challenges we face is the sharp decline in our ability to absorb information. This is partly due to the constant distractions and interruptions that come with modern technology, but also because of the stress and anxiety that many of us are experiencing.

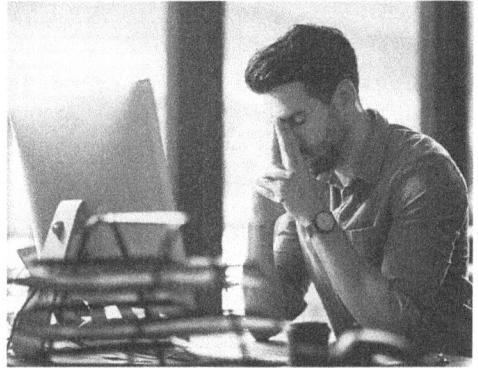

According to a recent Atlassian study, our ability to cope with change has plummeted to 50 per cent less than pre-pandemic levels.[11] The years of existing in a constant state of emergency due to the pandemic led to a depletion of our emergency reserves of energy and attention – our 'surge capacity'. As a result, we are now more stressed and less able to make clear decisions.[12] Studies have shown that stress can impair our cognitive abilities, including our decision-making skills, which can make it difficult to navigate change effectively.[13]

Another major challenge is the constant information overload and dwindling attention spans that we face. With so much information available to us on a 24/7 basis, it is nearly impossible to focus on the most important tasks and initiatives. This leads to a lack of clarity and direction, which can undermine change initiatives.

Many organisations are also facing intensified pressure to do more with less. This can create a culture of overwork and burnout, which can further hinder change initiatives. The conventional approach of trying to be everything to everyone, with multiple projects in flight, can often result in failure, inadequate resources and competing priorities.

To address these challenges, it is important to fight back against the pressure to do more with less. Instead, we should focus on doing less with less, but do it exceptionally well. This means consolidating projects and focusing on the most important initiatives.

Southwest Airlines is a great example. Small but mighty, its success is achieved by having a laser-like focus on a limited number of initiatives aligning with its business objectives. The company's leadership prioritises only a few key initiatives in areas such as customer service, operational efficiency and employee satisfaction, and has consistently invested in these areas over the years. Emphasis on 'consistently'. Southwest has been able to execute its strategy more effectively and efficiently than its competitors, maintaining a strong culture of innovation and continuous improvement.[14] Its success demonstrates that it is possible to achieve outstanding results with a smaller number of changes, as long as they are strategic and focus on core objectives.

By conserving our energy and resources we can take care of people's wellbeing while maximising our ROI and increasing the chances of success. This means we must be selective on the initiatives we greenlight, and invest in their success. Approving a dozen change initiatives and expecting them all to succeed is the definition of insanity. Change management is harder today due to various factors, but by understanding these challenges and adopting a more focused and strategic approach, we can overcome them and achieve successful change.

APPROVING A DOZEN CHANGE INITIATIVES AND EXPECTING THEM ALL TO SUCCEED IS THE DEFINITION OF INSANITY.

The attention economy

Back in 2017 Forbes reported that each of us is bombarded with an estimated 4,000 to 10,000 marketing messages per day.[15] How many messages do you think we're exposed to today?

Getting someone's attention is the first step to generating awareness of a change. Let's think about our attention spans for a moment. Sharing and consuming content has never been easier, but interest fades fast. Seconds later there is a new viral meme or news story vying for our attention. Global attention spans are narrowing and trends don't last as long as they used to. A 2013 Twitter global trend would last for an average of 17.5 hours, compared with a 2016 Twitter trend of only 11.9 hours. The latest data shows that in 2020, trending topics have a shelf life of 11 minutes.[16]

> # DON'T BE AFRAID TO GIVE UP THE GOOD TO GO FOR THE GREAT.
>
> ## JOHN D ROCKEFELLER

In 2000, our attention spans were averaging 12 seconds. Now scientists think our attention spans are around eight seconds – shorter than those of goldfish, which are able to focus on a task or object for nine seconds. Eeps! Scary stats.[17] The amount of time we spend on individual web pages has also decreased significantly, with research showing that the average time spent on a web page is just 15 seconds.[18]

We are bombarded with a never-ending stream of information, from social media notifications and emails to advertisements and news alerts. With the rise of smartphones and other mobile devices, our attention is constantly divided, resulting in a phenomenon known as continuous partial attention. This means that we are rarely fully engaged in any one task or activity.

The consequences of this attention fragmentation are significant, affecting not only our ability to perform tasks effectively but also our mental health. Studies have shown that the constant stimulation and distraction of the digital age can lead to increased stress, anxiety and even depression.[19]

The impact of these trends on change management is significant. With people's attention spans growing shorter, it has become increasingly challenging to communicate complex messages effectively. This is particularly true in the workplace, where employees are often juggling multiple tasks and responsibilities. If you want your changes to be understood, embraced and adopted, you must find innovative ways to capture and retain your audience's attention, such as using gamification or interactive content to make your message more engaging and memorable.

A company that has done this incredibly well is Apple. Known for its ability to simplify complex technological concepts and communicate them in a way that is easy for consumers to understand, its campaigns engage even non-tech-savvy consumers. Apple's product launches and keynotes are also carefully crafted to communicate complex concepts through visuals, metaphors and analogies. They use simple, straightforward language that doesn't take too much brainpower to digest. By simplifying the complex, Apple engages consumers and creates a strong emotional connection between people and its products.

> **THE GREATEST DISCOVERY OF ALL TIME IS THAT A PERSON CAN CHANGE HIS FUTURE BY MERELY CHANGING HIS ATTITUDE.**
>
> **OPRAH WINFREY**

Have you ever witnessed a product launch day at an Apple store? The queue often stretches for many blocks, with some people camping out overnight to secure their place. Simplifying the complex has helped the company become one of the most valuable brands in the world.

The attention economy is a crucial aspect of change management. With people's attention becoming increasingly fragmented and smaller, it's important to understand the dynamics involved and find ways to capture and retain attention in non-spammy ways.

WITH PEOPLE'S ATTENTION BECOMING INCREASINGLY FRAGMENTED AND SMALLER, IT'S IMPORTANT TO UNDERSTAND THE DYNAMICS INVOLVED AND FIND WAYS TO CAPTURE AND RETAIN ATTENTION IN NON-SPAMMY WAYS.

Why change flops with workplace stress

The world is getting more competitive. Each year it seems budgets are tightened and teams get smaller. We're expected to do more with less. We have less people, less money and less time to meet big goals and achieve even bigger results.

It should come as no surprise then that the success rate for digital transformation is even lower than that for non-tech change initiatives such as business process re-engineering or an organisational restructure. McKinsey has quoted the success rates of digital transformation as consistently less than 30 per cent.[20]

This low success rate would be unacceptable elsewhere. Can you imagine if a skydiving company only successfully landed three out of 100 customer dives? Splat! Or a political candidate getting 5 per cent of the votes then expecting to be president? Can anyone say 'out of touch with reality'? People would be rioting in the streets.

Yet when it comes to digital transformation, these stats are accepted, ignored and hidden within giant spreadsheets and reports. These numbers won't change if *we* don't change. Want a different result? Pursue a different outcome. It's common sense if you ask me.

> **THE GOOD NEWS IS THE EMOTIONAL UPS AND DOWNS OF TRANSFORMATIONS DON'T LAST FOREVER; BUT THEY CAN STILL TAKE A TOLL ON OUR MENTAL WELLBEING AND PERFORMANCE.**

Large digital transformation initiatives are like an emotional roller-coaster ride. Once you're on, you often feel like you're never getting off – and you're fighting anxiety and nausea when you see the double upside-down loops! The good news is the emotional ups and downs of transformations don't last forever; but they can still take a toll on our mental wellbeing and performance.

Vast amounts of research point to the huge problems associated with work-related stress, and I've seen evidence of this in my career, too. According to the Australian Human Rights Commission, Australian businesses lose over $6.5 billion annually by failing to provide early intervention for employees with mental health conditions, with a survey indicating 25 per cent of workers have taken time off for stress-related reasons.[21] Even 15 years ago, workplace stress was already costing the Australian economy $14.81 billion a year. Stress-related presenteeism and absenteeism are directly costing Australian employers $10.11 billion a year, and 3.2 days per worker are lost each year to workplace stress.[22]

This needs to – pardon the pun – change, and change fast. We know we're looking down the barrel of faster, more complex and overlapping technological, environmental and economic change. When change management is absent, changes become a source of distress and worry.

If we aspire for our workplaces to contribute to healthier, happier and more enriched lives, we must monitor employee emotional wellbeing. We must invest in prevention now, to avoid paying more for a cure in the future.

Let's look at what some of the world's leading organisations are doing about workplace stress.

Build a culture of resilience and wellness

Unilever has built a single global model for employee wellbeing that is used across the business. More than one-third of its entire workforce of 155,000 people has attended its 'Thrive' workshops for support in building a personal wellbeing plan. Unilever is also trialling a well-being app for employees to access health and wellbeing information or urgent assistance. Employee wellbeing has become part of the culture and what the organisation stands for.

Building a culture of resilience and wellness is not an insurmountable task, even for a company of significant size and global footprint. Find opportunities within your existing or new digital transformation to make employee wellness the 'hero'; the benefits to the business and individuals will be significant.

Equip leaders to detect emotional distress

The Woolworths I am Here program aims to take the stigma out of mental illness. The voluntary program has trained more than 20,000 people in looking out for mental health red flags, both in themselves and in colleagues, and how to encourage those struggling to get help. While programs such as this should be mandatory for all senior leaders, it is an excellent example of one of Australia's biggest employers making mental health a priority.

Explore ways to drive participation in mental health training programs in your own workplace. Mandating compulsory attendance is obviously one approach, but there are others that use more carrot, less stick!

Leaders must create awareness and develop ninja-like observational skills. I have observed situations where the fast-paced frenetic organisational culture meant mental health warning signs were ignored. It was expected people would just 'power through'. The outcome (surprise, freakin' surprise) was that an employee had a breakdown and was on stress leave for months. This could have been avoided, or minimised, through regular managerial check-ins and more frequent timeouts.

Go bottom-up

Google's employees started a program called Blue Dot: a peer-to-peer listening program. It enables Google's people to become compassionate listeners for those who might be struggling with work or family life, anxiety or other mental health–related issues. There are currently 400 volunteer Blue Dot listeners, and they are recognised by the blue sticker stuck on their desk or name tag. While the project is not tracking any adoption data, Blue Dot representatives see the initiative as effective and popular.

Employee wellness is everybody's concern. A bottom-up program such as Google's can be just as effective as a top-down program. Ultimately, people need to be encouraged to speak up if they're not feeling okay, and feel they can ask for help without being judged. Leaders have a responsibility to role model, advocate for and champion this.

FAILURE IS NOT FATAL, BUT FAILURE TO CHANGE MIGHT BE.

JOHN WOODEN

To flip the statistics of digital transformation failure, we need a new approach to managing change of all kinds.

Look beyond the tech

Unless we stop traversing the path of least resistance – which is autopilot spending on more tech – we'll be plagued by single-digit success rates for a lifetime.

I'll let you in on a secret: it's not the tech that's failed. It's not the processes that are broken. It's the people side of transformation that's been neglected.

Our love affair with the latest and greatest technologies means we've forgotten the tool is only as powerful as the people who are using it.

Here's an example: Microsoft Excel. For the small minority who are superusers it is an incredibly powerful tool that can provide insights, do custom reporting, influence key decisions (which can unlock record profitability) and more. For everyone else, myself included, it's more like a calculator!

I'm sure we all know someone who upgrades to the newest phone every two years without fail yet doesn't make full use of the additional capabilities the latest version brings. The same thing occurs in organisations.

You don't need the shiny new toy. You need to make sure your people know about, want to and have the skills to play with your current tech.

If every organisation simply invested time and resources into making sure its people understood how to get the most out of its

> **EVERY SUCCESSFUL ORGANISATION HAS TO MAKE THE TRANSITION FROM A WORLD DEFINED PRIMARILY BY REPETITION TO ONE PRIMARILY DEFINED BY CHANGE. THIS IS THE BIGGEST TRANSFORMATION IN THE STRUCTURE OF HOW HUMANS WORK TOGETHER SINCE THE AGRICULTURAL REVOLUTION.**
>
> **BILL DRAYTON**

current technology suite, we'd be amazed at the results and performance that could be achieved.

PAUSE AND REFLECT

- Why do you think change initiatives often fail to deliver the intended outcomes? Reflect on the common factors and challenges that contribute to the high failure rate, including resistance to change, inadequate communication and insufficient learning and unlearning within your organisation.

- How open are you/is your organisation to relearning and unlearning established ways of thinking and doing? What strategies could you employ to overcome the barriers to this? Explore potential solutions such as creating a supportive learning environment, promoting a growth mindset, encouraging experimentation and risk-taking and fostering a culture of curiosity and exploration.

- Think of your own behaviour. Are there some unproductive or unhealthy habits you need to unlearn? How would you go about this?

CHAPTER 3

SPORTS CARS SNEAKERS AND STILETTOS

Humour me for a moment. Imagine the most powerful, sexy, high-performance sports car in the world. Close your eyes for a few seconds and conjure the image in your mind. Got it?

That's right –

The Toyota Prius!

Okay, jokes aside – I have much better taste than that (don't send me hate mail, Prius drivers). I'm sure most readers had something like a red Ferrari in mind.

Now visualise your granny driving this powerful beast. If Formula 1 driver Sebastian Vettel was behind the wheel of the not-so-sexy Prius, do you think he'd beat Granny around the track? Yup, he definitely would.

Even if I have a Speedo Fastskin suit on (Michael Phelps wore the Fastskin II and won eight gold medals in the 2008 Beijing Olympics) I'm not going to outswim Ian Thorpe. And a couch potato in the most advanced, high-tech Nikes won't be winning any marathons.

Despite all this, executives think future fitness is determined by their tech stack. A tech stack is the combination of applications, programs and systems an organisation uses to build and run an application or project. Many a C-suite executive has told me they can simply 'out-tech' the humans in their organisations; that getting the best, newest, most advanced tools will make up for chronic underinvestment in their people.

JUST AS A HIGH-PERFORMANCE SPORTS CAR NEEDS A SKILLED DRIVER TO MAKE THE MOST OF ITS CAPABILITIES, SO TOO DO COMPANIES NEED SKILLED EMPLOYEES TO MAKE THE MOST OF THEIR TECHNOLOGY INVESTMENTS.

The metaphor of a granny driving a powerful sports car illustrates the importance of investing in people rather than just technology. Just as a high-performance sports car needs a skilled driver to make the most of its capabilities, so too do companies need skilled employees to make the most of their technology investments.

Executives often think that technology is the key to success and that investing in the latest tools and systems will automatically lead to better results. This mistaken thinking is pervasive in leadership ranks and overlooks the importance of the human element. While technology can certainly enhance productivity and efficiency, it's the people who ultimately make that happen.

Investing in people means providing the necessary training and development opportunities to help employees improve their skills and knowledge. It means creating a culture that values and supports employees, and empowers them to make decisions and take ownership of their work. It means recognising individual employees' contributions and fostering a sense of teamwork and collaboration.

By neglecting to invest in people, executives are not only missing out on the full potential of their technology investments, they also risk creating a disengaged and unmotivated workforce. A study by the Society for Human Resource Management found employee recognition is a top driver of employee engagement. It found 86 per cent of companies with employee recognition programs reported an increase in employee happiness, and 85 per cent reported an increase in employee engagement.[23] Gallup echoes this, with its study finding the main reason for low employee engagement is a lack of recognition and praise from managers.[24]

It's not rocket science; we're human *beings*, not human *doings*. Gartner found 82 per cent of employees feel that they are not recognised for their work as often as they should be, and that those receiving recognition for their work are more engaged, more likely to stay with the company and more productive than those who do not.[25]

News flash: employees who feel undervalued or underappreciated will not go the extra mile or take on additional responsibilities.

In short, while technology is important, it's not a silver bullet. The key to success lies in finding the right balance, and integrating technology and people. The smart money is on companies that invest in both.

Stacking it up

We've talked about the tech stack. Now, here's a new concept: what about the people stack?

Picture an actual 'people stack'. Do you know the game of Jenga, which involves players removing blocks from a tower without causing it to crumble? Picture giant human Jenga blocks stacked on top of each other. Just like in the game, if you remove the wrong block – the wrong skill, the wrong mindset – the tower of transformation will come crumbling down.

The people stack concept is relatively new but it's becoming increasingly important to consider in today's rapidly changing business environment. Think of it as the combination of skills, ethnicities, knowledge, emotions and personality traits connected via shared organisational values. Just as a tech stack is critical to building and running an application or project, a people stack is critical to how an organisation performs.

> # I CAN'T CHANGE THE DIRECTION OF THE WIND, BUT I CAN ADJUST MY SAILS TO ALWAYS REACH MY DESTINATION.
>
> JIMMY DEAN

The people stack is all about building the right team with the right mix of skills and traits to achieve the organisation's goals. It's not just about hiring the best and brightest, but about creating a team that is diverse, adaptable and aligned with the organisation's culture, vision and mission.

Executives who focus too much on the tech stack and not enough on the people stack risk overlooking the most critical component of their organisation's success: the ability to adapt and pivot quickly. This requires a team that is agile, innovative and resilient.

Executives don't spend a lot of time – actually, I'd argue, *any* time – thinking about how to best customise a people stack that is aligned with their organisational culture, vision and mission. Instead they spend an inordinate amount of time worrying about malware or the metaverse. Yes, these are important issues, especially when we've seen many giant organisations splashed on newspaper front pages for failing to take cybersecurity measures to protect their customers. But if those organisations had the right components in their people stack, these types of oversights would be greatly minimised.

Building the right people stack requires a deep understanding of the organisation's mission, culture and values, as well as a focus on developing and nurturing talent. This includes investing in training and development programs, fostering a culture of learning and growth, and creating opportunities for employees to take on new challenges and expand their skills.

While the tech stack is certainly important, it is the people stack that is the true foundation of any successful organisation. Executives who invest in building the right people stack will be better positioned to navigate today's challenges and achieve tomorrow's successes.

> MY THEORY ON LIFE IS THAT LIFE IS BEAUTIFUL. LIFE DOESN'T CHANGE. YOU HAVE A DAY, AND A NIGHT, AND A MONTH, AND A YEAR. WE PEOPLE CHANGE – WE CAN BE MISERABLE OR WE CAN BE HAPPY. IT'S WHAT YOU MAKE OF YOUR LIFE.
>
> MOHAMMED BIN RASHID AL MAKTOUM

The executives who share my view are many. Jeff Bezos, founder and former CEO of Amazon, has spoken extensively about the importance of hiring the right people. He once said, 'I'd rather interview 50 people and not hire anyone than hire the wrong person.' Bezos believes having the right people is essential to achieving Amazon's long-term goals and staying competitive in a rapidly changing market.

Microsoft CEO Satya Nadella has emphasised the importance of having a growth mindset and a culture that values learning and development. He said, 'We need to have a culture that allows us to constantly grow and learn.' He believes that having the right people and a culture that supports growth and development is essential for Microsoft to continue innovating and staying ahead of the curve.

Jenga in reverse

There is a tendency to push people out of organisations – either firing them or making their position redundant – when they are not meeting expectations, rather than investing in them to improve their contribution. This often leads to low morale, distrust and lost productivity, not to mention the extra costs involved in hiring a new person.

The cost varies depending on a variety of factors, such as the level of the position, the industry and the location, however the US Society for Human Resource Management (SHRM) says the average cost of replacing an employee is between six and nine months of the employee's salary.[26] This includes both direct and indirect costs associated with hiring and training a new employee, as well as the loss of productivity during the transition period.

The costs of replacing an employee add up fast, considering they include expenses such as:

- **Advertising costs:** To attract new candidates, the company may need to advertise the job opening on job boards, social media or other platforms. These costs can vary depending on the advertising strategy.

- **Recruitment fees:** If the company uses a recruitment agency to help find new candidates, there may be fees associated with this service.

- **Time spent on recruiting and hiring:** HR personnel and hiring managers will spend time reviewing résumés, conducting interviews and communicating with candidates throughout the process.

- **Onboarding costs:** Once a new employee is hired, there may be costs associated with onboarding and training, such as orientation sessions and training materials.

- **Lost productivity:** When an employee is fired or made redundant, there is often a gap in productivity as the company works to replace that person and the new incumbent gets up to speed. This lost productivity can be costly, especially if the position is critical to the company's operations.

I argue we should critically evaluate how we build and maintain our people stack. Instead of removing people, the emphasis should be on expanding their skills, experiences and emotional intelligence.

But how do you go about this? A starting point is to get a picture of the complete stack of skills, experiences, views and cultures necessary to make your transformation successful. This stack should include book smarts, people smarts and emotional smarts. Then consider whether the differences between the people in the stack are complementary and what could make the stack stronger and more robust.

Is your people stack fit for the present, one year from now or five years from now? How will you develop the necessary skills if they cannot be bought? The role of emotional intelligence in improving interpersonal relationships, both in and out of the workplace, must be recognised. The benefits of emotional intelligence include being able to better understand nonverbal cues, adjust behaviour, make good decisions and become a respected leader.

In today's fast-paced and complex world, the ability to manage emotions and make sound decisions is crucial for success both in the home and the office. Developing cognitive and emotional intelligence

can significantly enhance our ability to build interpersonal relationships and become an effective leader.

To help strengthen thought processes and decision-making capabilities, I suggest investing in professional development programs
that focus on critical thinking, problem-solving and decision-making.
These programs can teach people how to analyse complex information, evaluate different options and make informed decisions based
on data and logic. Workshops on effective communication and
collaboration can also help individuals work better in teams, share
ideas and make collective decisions faster and with less friction.

To manage emotions, mindfulness techniques such as meditation and
deep breathing, and emotional cue cards to self-identify the emotions
you're feeling is extremely helpful. We're not taught this in schools,
and certain ethnic backgrounds don't talk about emotions – ever. It's
useful to bring physical tools in to help facilitate these conversations.
These techniques can help regulate emotions, reduce stress and
improve wellbeing. It is also essential to create a culture of psychological safety in the workplace, where individuals feel comfortable
sharing their thoughts and feelings without fear of judgement or retribution.

Leaders must invest in their own emotional intelligence and lead by
example. By demonstrating empathy, active listening and emotional
self-awareness, leaders can create a
more positive and supportive work environment, which can ultimately lead to
increased productivity and engagement.

By fortifying the people stack with the
right skills, experiences and emotional
intelligence, organisations can accelerate

**THERE IS NO SEPARATION
OF MIND AND EMOTIONS;
EMOTIONS, THINKING, AND
LEARNING ARE ALL LINKED.**

ERIC JENSEN

their transformation and achieve success. Start compiling the right people, not the right tools, and you *will* accelerate your transformation. Because it is people who change, not organisations. Transformation is only possible when individual change occurs at scale.

Two transformative traits

I've had to build a change practice from scratch. I mean, change is hard. Changing yourself is often challenging; imagine changing the behaviour of an organisation with tens of thousands of employees? If anyone tells you it's easy, they're either delusional or in denial. Humans are hard-wired to resist change. It served us well when we were in danger of being eaten by dinosaurs, but now, not so much.

When I'm hiring a *dream team* that possesses the 'x factor' to ignite and inspire change, I'm looking for two key traits: *openness* to change and assuming *positive* intent. These traits enable transformation to come alive as people explore and experiment with new technology.

Openness helps people feel more satisfied with their life, lowers stress and supports good physical health. How an employee feels about their life directly impacts how they show up at work. If employees are open to new experiences, it's likely they'll feel more motivated in their work and tasks.

HOW AN EMPLOYEE FEELS ABOUT THEIR LIFE DIRECTLY IMPACTS HOW THEY SHOW UP AT WORK.

Defaulting to assuming positive intent is healthy in any kind of a relationship. As a co-worker, leader, colleague, friend or romantic partner, assuming positive intent builds trust and creates a space where it's safe to be vulnerable and honest. Defaulting to positive intent is harder to do because we remember negatives more than positives: for every one negative experience or interaction, we need five positive ones to counteract the impact.[27]

Let's look at some ways to measure these traits.

One way to measure an individual's openness to change is to use a personality assessment tool, such as one that assesses the Big Five personality traits. Openness is one of the Big Five traits, based on an individual's level of imagination, creativity and willingness to try new things. Another way to measure openness to change is through performance evaluations and feedback sessions. These sessions can provide insight into how an employee responds to new challenges and changes in the workplace. For example, if an employee consistently shows a willingness to take on new tasks, and approaches problems with a creative mindset, it may indicate higher openness to change.

It is more difficult to measure the assumption of positive intent, as this is more a mindset or attitude than a tangible behaviour. However, one way to assess an individual's tendency to assume positive intent is through their communication style. Individuals who assume positive intent are more likely to give others the benefit of the doubt and approach conversations with a cooperative and open-minded tone.

Another way to measure this trait is through feedback from colleagues or superiors. Asking for feedback on how an individual approaches difficult situations and conversations may provide insights into whether the person tends to assume positive intent or not. Self-reflection and introspection can also be helpful in identifying and improving this trait.

> FOR PEOPLE WHO HAD CURVE BALLS THROWN AT THEM, IT IS EASIER TO DIGEST CHANGE AND DIGEST CHANGE IN OTHER PEOPLE. CHANGE ONLY SCARES THE SMALL-MINDED.
>
> CASEY AFFLECK

Individuals who work on developing a positive mindset and approach to communication can improve their ability to assume positive intent in all aspects of their work. It's hard, but not impossible.

People with these characteristics, armed with the right technology, can create a movement that will penetrate each layer of an organisation.

The secret sauce of change

If I had a dollar for every time someone asked what kind of leadership traits get people paying attention and changing faster, I'd be retired by now. There is a secret sauce that makes people want to change, to follow, to listen, to adopt. Let me tell you about a time I experienced this for myself.

I admit I am often resistant to changing my own behaviour. I'd like to tell you about a man who was able to get me to do things differently, where others have failed. His strategies can be applied to organisations as well as operating rooms.

Seven years ago I had an accident that saw me rupture two out of the three ligaments in my left ankle. I knew it was bad when I couldn't stand up on my own, and didn't argue when I was ushered into the emergency room.

Post accident I saw a string of physiotherapists to help get my ankle back to normal – and because it was now significantly weaker, I would have recurring sprains every few months. It sucked. It hurt. It annoyed the heck out of me. I should mention I have a less-than-stellar track record with physios and acting on their advice. Why? I get bored standing on one leg, and I often believe I've healed faster than what I actually have. Oh, and I'm stubborn. I don't ice or elevate as much as I should and I certainly don't rest.

My ankle is still not as strong as it used to be; nowhere near it. I was advised to get reconstructive surgery, but I like to swim upstream. I have accepted a lifetime of being extra careful walking on cobblestone paths, never again being a regular pavement pounder (I liken long-distance running to torture anyway) and having a limited shoe collection, free of 12-centimetre stilettos.

Most physios I've seen have said to me: 'Friska, I can tell you're not icing and elevating every two hours like I advised. You need to do this. If you don't, your ankle will remain swollen and you'll struggle to go about your daily life. I can't start the rehabilitation exercises while it's still swollen. Are you taping it like I told you? You have to do this. I will see the difference next time you come in. There's no point making another appointment if you don't do what I say.'

My response? 'I know. I know. I know. I'll do better.'

And then I leave. And nothing changes. I do a Houdini and disappear, never returning to the same physio. When I was being 'good', I iced and elevated maybe twice a day versus the prescribed two to three hours. I just couldn't follow what the physios prescribed.

Then I moved interstate for my career. I found a new physio called Matt. My first appointment began like they always do; but then, everything changed.

Matt: Friska, you have strong muscles. I can tell by your right leg. And great balance too! Maybe you run or do yoga? That's more than the average person. This will make recovery much quicker for you.

Me: Oh, really? Yes, I've been practising yoga consistently for years. And I run . . . not as much now because of the ankle but I try to get out for a short one weekly.

Matt: I can tell. Those are good habits to get into; well done. Now, I see your left ankle is still swollen and much weaker than the other. But since you are so careful with your health, we will be able to help regain its strength and definitely prevent recurring sprains. But we will have to persist and battle through together.

Me: Yes! Let's partner together! How?

Matt: Here's what I am thinking. First, I want you to see your progress. I am going to measure the extent of the resistance you can push against, and your ankle's flexibility. When you come back for your next appointment, we can check your progress to see how we are doing. What do you think?

Me: Sounds good. Do you think I can be back to wearing stilettos without a reconstructive operation?

Matt: Yes, definitely! Scar tissue takes time to heal. You'll need patience, but eventually it will subside.

Firstly, we'll have an array of strengthening exercises for you to do each day. Just ten minutes while you're watching TV, brushing your teeth, working at your desk . . . that will really help.

Secondly, I'm going to leave you untaped so you can get used to getting around unassisted.

Thirdly, I'll use the therapeutic ultrasound machine each time you come in to help with the swelling.

Lastly, I am going to give you some tape, so when you are going hiking or feeling a bit wobbly, you can get used to taping it yourself. You won't need me all the time.

SINCE WE CANNOT CHANGE REALITY, LET US CHANGE THE EYES WHICH SEE REALITY.

NIKOS KAZANTZAKIS

Me: Okay, I can do ten minutes a day. I could do more if I consciously focus on it.

Matt: Absolutely! I have no doubt. When you come back we will compare measurements and see how we did. And if you're pushed for time, just focus on the first two exercises I give you. They have the most impact. I understand life gets busy.

Me: Okay! I hope every week I will make progress.

Matt: I know you will!

I did my exercises almost religiously after that fateful first appointment.

Matt achieved something powerful with me that day in his office. I have reflected on why I chose to listen to him; why he was able to cut through when no-one else had.

We always want to change people. We want to help. To fix. To improve. We advise, problem-solve, suggest, try to change someone for their own good. Our heart is in the right place.

But unless they want to change, nothing we say or do will influence their behaviour.

Here are some ideas my experience with Matt taught me about how to positively change someone's behaviour.

Step 1: Invoke pride

Matt started out by invoking feelings of pride in me. He noticed the strength and flexibility of my right ankle, and mentioned it was better than most people's. This immediately made me feel proud of what I had done, instead of guilty about what I had not. It made a major difference. Pride makes us want to do more – it makes us feel powerful and we want to live up to that feeling.

How do you make others feel proud of themselves? It's pretty simple: you point out the positives; you praise them for what they are doing right; and you illustrate a self-fulfilling prophecy.

Step 2: Engage

Matt used the word 'we' more than 'you'. His approach was to involve me, not to tell me. The outcome was that I felt it was truly a team effort. In a professional context, involvement and adopting a collaborative approach is a surefire way to generate engagement, commitment and buy-in. It can be a painful process, and is definitely more effort-intensive and slow, but the dividends it pays will help you in the long run.

To engage people, say 'we' not 'you'; involve, don't instruct; and buddy up with other people to change as a collective.

Step 3: Track progress

The next thing Matt did was catalogue my progress. He took measurements of my ankle and how far I could bend and flex. This gave me a benchmark – it's like seeing how much you have in your savings account or weighing yourself. Specific, measurable goals are always easier to achieve. I could see my measurements each week. I competed only with myself and wanted to improve on them each visit. Matt defined the goal posts. Previous physios would just give me exercises and I had no way of tracking whether they made any difference!

Small wins, visibly and regularly celebrated, are a powerful motivator. Define a measurable benchmark, track progress and make it easy to visualise change.

Step 4: Provide tools

The last thing Matt did was give me specific tools and steps. I had heard all of these before, but not in such a direct, prescriptive way. When other physios gave me tools they felt like orders; but the way Matt described the tools made them feel like weapons. He broke what I needed to do down into manageable actions and promised a measurable outcome. He empathised with the busyness of modern life and provided a shortcut option without making me feel like I was copping out if I took it. I was hooked.

Give your people steps to follow, provide helpful tools in an empathetic way, and show a clear path to change.

GIVE YOUR PEOPLE STEPS TO FOLLOW, PROVIDE HELPFUL TOOLS IN AN EMPATHETIC WAY, AND SHOW A CLEAR PATH TO CHANGE.

Matt's approach was very different to traditional behaviour-change strategies such as exerting pressure and guilt tripping. It goes against our instincts to engage people in this way when we want them to change, but it actually gets results without making people feel bad in the process. Have you heard of positive psychology and appreciative inquiry? It's about more carrot, less stick. We all have behaviours we know we should change; it's refreshing to receive a bit of compassionate help sometimes.

(And by the way, I've maintained my ankle strength, have been super careful on soft or declining ground and continue to have zero interest in becoming an elite runner. I have quite happily gotten by sans reconstructive surgery. Oh, and I've settled for eight-centimetre heels.)

PAUSE AND REFLECT

- What key skills and competencies are required in your organisation for it to thrive? Do you think these will change over the next five years? Reflect on the evolving demands of the business landscape and consider the technical, interpersonal and cognitive skills that will be essential for success.

- How can your organisation foster a culture of continuous learning and development to support people through transformation? Consider the role of leadership, training programs, mentorship and opportunities for growth in nurturing employees' skills, capabilities and career progression.

- Think of who's in your current people stack. How can you align their individual personalities and strengths – now and during times of change? How can you maximise their potential to contribute to the overall success of the organisation? Compare the skills and competencies of those people to what's needed to drive future success. What are the gaps? Where are they? How will you close them?

CHAPTER 4

ALL ABOUT EXTENDED REALITY

Now that we've covered the origins of change management and the historical lacklustre results of transformation, and thought deeply about the people stack that will support your organisation through change, let's move on to examine some specifics.

Extended reality (ER) is a technology that adds digital elements to our physical environment, thus enhancing our experience of the world. ER includes both augmented reality (AR) and virtual reality (VR), and it has been around for several decades. The advancements in technology and the widespread availability of smartphones and other devices have made ER more accessible and more commonly known.

AR is the use of digital information, such as graphics, sounds and GPS data, to enhance our perception of the physical world. AR can be used in a variety of settings such as retail, gaming, education and healthcare. For example, AR can be used to display product information or pricing in a store, to create interactive educational experiences, or to provide training simulations in healthcare.

VR, on the other hand, is a fully immersive experience in a digital environment that is designed to simulate reality. VR can be used for entertainment purposes, such as gaming and movies, but it can also have practical applications in education, training and therapy.

The potential applications of ER are vast and, as the technology continues to evolve, we are likely to see even more innovative and creative uses. For example, ER could be used to create immersive experiences for travellers, to enhance remote communication and collaboration, or to provide new forms of entertainment.

As ER becomes more prevalent, it is important for individuals and organisations to understand its capabilities and potential applications. This includes exploring ways to integrate ER into existing products and services, as well as considering new ways to use the technology to enhance user experiences.

ER has the potential to transform the way we experience the world around us. As with any emerging technology, it is important to stay informed and to consider the ethical implications of its use.

ER's infancy

Many people think ER is relatively new, but it's not.

Way back in the '90s, movies such as *The Lawnmower Man*, *Virtuosity* and *Existenz* all featured elements of ER. Remember that era? Nickelodeon ruled TV with shows such as *Rugrats* and *Rocket Power*; *The All-New Mickey Mouse Club* kicked off its sixth season in 1993 with Britney Spears, Justin Timberlake, Christina Aguilera and Ryan Gosling; Furbies were *the* toy on every kid's Christmas wishlist; Warner Bros stores thrived then dived (thanks to the previously mentioned Time Warner and AOL merger); tweens were preoccupied with feeding their Tamagotchis; and *Friends* debuted on NBC.

Do you remember the mid 2010s Pokémon GO craze that had people out 'hunting' for these mythical creatures? Participants got off their sofas and benefited from some sunshine and exercise. Unfortunately, though, some people were so immersed in the ER world they sustained injuries, tripping over footpaths and even walking in front of cars due to inattention.

Yep, ER has been around for a while; but real-world adoption has been slow. After the introduction of ER technology to the world, nothing happened for 17 years. Then it started to go mainstream. In fact, the global ER market is expected to exceed US$1.1 trillion by 2030, expanding 45 per cent from 2020 to 2030.[28]

> **THE SECRET OF CHANGE IS TO FOCUS ALL OF YOUR ENERGY NOT ON FIGHTING THE OLD, BUT ON BUILDING THE NEW.**
>
> **SOCRATES**

Growth of ER

A shift in focus within the ER industry towards consumers' needs, wants and fears has led to significant advancements in the adoption of the technology. Prioritising human needs and designing technology around them has made ER technology more accessible and user-friendly.

This shift towards people-centric design has been made possible by a variety of tools and approaches such as design thinking, user experience design, customer experience, empathy mapping and more. The common thread between these approaches is that they prioritise understanding the end users' needs, wants and pain points before jumping into the design.

> **YOU CANNOT CHANGE THE PEOPLE AROUND YOU, BUT YOU CAN CHANGE THE PEOPLE YOU CHOOSE TO BE AROUND.**
>
> **UNKNOWN**

By doing this, the ER industry has been able to develop more meaningful and impactful applications of the technology. It has been able to create experiences that are not only visually stimulating but also serve a real purpose for consumers.

In the healthcare industry, ER is being used to improve patient outcomes by simulating surgeries and training medical professionals. In education, ER is being used to create immersive learning environments that help students better understand complex concepts. In entertainment, ER is being used to create more engaging and interactive experiences for audiences.

Overall, the shift towards people-first design in the ER industry has been a game changer. They started building bridges, connecting people's needs and wants to create a solution, instead of dams, where the industry prioritised product and problems.

ER and empathy

Empathy builds openness to change.

Think of someone you know, or perhaps someone famous you don't personally know, who has a strong reputation as an empathetic leader of change. What are the visible empathy indicators?

Usually, we know a leader is empathetic when they seek to understand how and why people are reacting to or behaving around the upcoming changes. They recognise that just because people have different experiences, expectations and reactions, that doesn't mean those people are wrong or invalid. Empathetic leaders approach differences with curiosity, not contempt.

I've found that one of the most effective strategies to manage change is to reduce people's fear of the unknown. And the first step towards doing that is to gain their trust. You can only start building trust by operating from a place of empathy.

The co-existence of vulnerability and empathy builds a solid foundation upon which you can understand others' perspectives, gain trust and move forward – together – into the unknown.

Today's world requires companies to innovate and transform quickly to remain competitive. Leaders looking to take a more empathetic approach for better change outcomes must incorporate vulnerability and caring to enable faster, more holistic transformation.

> **CHANGE WILL NOT COME IF WE WAIT FOR SOME OTHER PERSON OR SOME OTHER TIME. WE ARE THE ONES WE'VE BEEN WAITING FOR. WE ARE THE CHANGE THAT WE SEEK.**
>
> **BARACK OBAMA**

Think about leaders who have done this successfully. Jacinda Ardern, former Prime Minister of New Zealand, is known for her empathetic and caring leadership style. She demonstrated this through her response to the Christchurch mosque shootings in 2019 and again in the 2020 COVID-19 pandemic. When she speaks, the world listens; she knows her stakeholders intimately and therefore talks in their language.

Dr Vishal Sikka, former CEO of Infosys, a multinational information technology company based in India, believes in the power of empathy to foster innovation and creativity. He has encouraged his employees to think beyond their roles and embrace new ideas.

Christine Lagarde, President of the European Central Bank, has advocated for policies that prioritise citizens' wellbeing and emphasised the importance of diversity and inclusion in the workplace. She has also encouraged collaboration and cooperation among European leaders to address the challenges facing the region.

Feike Sijbesma, former CEO of DSM, a global science-based company based in the Netherlands, is known for his purpose-driven leadership style. He believes in using business as a force for good and has implemented several initiatives aimed at improving employee wellbeing, as well as wellbeing in the communities in which DSM operates.

WHEN WE ARE NO LONGER ABLE TO CHANGE A SITUATION, WE ARE CHALLENGED TO CHANGE OURSELVES.

VIKTOR E FRANKL

This empathetic approach – the ability to step into another's shoes and truly see the world as they experience it – is what skyrocketed the penetration of ER around the world.

We can leverage ER to encourage more empathetic decision-making. A recent study found that VR was just as effective at eliciting empathy as other empathy-inducing activities.[29] The research described what they called an 'embodied' experience. An embodied experience attempts to recreate the experience of the target group to bring the participant closer to the target's lived experience. They used an example of a VR experience (being virtually present with a woman who must carry water from a distant source to provide for her family), and contrasted this with an embodied experience (actually carrying heavy water jugs for 10 minutes).

A wide range of VR experiences is available, offering different levels of interaction and aiming to promote positive societal impact. One notable example is the VR experience 1000 Cut Journey, where users assume the role of Michael Sterling, a Black man, and encounter racism while engaging in daily activities. Users can interact with the virtual environment by performing actions such as opening doors and picking up objects through a controller. Another example is Clouds over Sidra, a less interactive experience that immerses users in a 360-degree video, allowing them to follow the daily life of 12-year-old Sidra, a refugee camp resident.

The field of VR continues to evolve with innovative designers world-wide creating new and diverse experiences. In 2016, the prominent VR company Oculus launched the VR for Good initiative, which aimed to encourage designers to develop content with a positive social impact. In 2017 HTC VIVE, a leading competitor, introduced its own program called VR for Impact, offering a US$10 million fund to support the creation of VR experiences for social good. Charitable organisations have also embraced VR as a tool for their fundraising campaigns, recognising its potential to engage audiences – to enable them to virtually and metaphorically walk a mile in another's shoes – and create immersive storytelling experiences.

ER has shown promise in the realm of chronic pain treatment and mental health. Immersing patients in VR-powered simulations offers them fresh perspectives on their pain, potentially leading to their ability to explore and experiment with improved coping mechanisms. VR has also proven valuable in addressing mental health challenges as it allows individuals to confront and manage their fears and anxieties in a controlled environment, safe from 'real' physical harm. The therapeutic potential of VR in these areas opens new possibilities for enhancing patient experiences and improving overall wellbeing.

PAUSE AND REFLECT

- In what ways can ER technologies, such as VR and AR, enhance empathy in the context of transformation? Reflect on the potential of these technologies to create immersive and empathetic experiences that foster understanding, collaboration and perspective-taking among stakeholders.

- How can you/your organisation promote empathy-driven decision-making during transformation? Consider the role of virtual simulations, interactive scenarios and immersive storytelling in helping leaders and employees empathise with the challenges, opportunities and experiences of different stakeholders affected by the transformation process.

- Are you building bridges instead of dams? How can you/ your organisation default to seeking to understand versus being in problem-solving mode?

CHAPTER 5

MAXIMISING POTENTIAL

ER technology offers opportunities for various industries to reimagine the way they operate. For instance, in the tourism industry, ER can transport travellers to different locations, allowing them to experience destinations in a whole new way. Imagine exploring the Leaning Tower of Pisa in a straightened form, witnessing the Sphinx with its nose attached, or even parting the Red Sea with Moses. ER technology can create virtual experiences that are not only fun and exciting, but also educational.

ER technology has the potential to transform the tourism industry in the face of unprecedented challenges such as the COVID-19 pandemic. As travel restrictions and lockdowns forced the industry to come to a halt, businesses could use ER technology to maintain relationships with customers and introduce their offerings to prospective visitors. Virtual 3D tours of popular tourist destinations such as Rome, Prague and Santorini were being offered as Airbnb experiences in 2021. This type of immersive technology could be the key to attracting new markets and helping businesses in the tourism industry to cope with challenging times.

Beyond tourism, ER technology has the power to transform various other industries such as healthcare, education, entertainment and manufacturing, to name a few. In healthcare, ER can provide realistic training simulations for medical professionals, allowing them to hone their skills without putting patients at risk. Imagine a doctor performing surgery with the help of a mixed reality interface (MRITF). The technology could project a 3D image of the patient's body in real time, allowing the doctor to visualise the procedure and make more accurate incisions. This could potentially reduce the risk of complications and improve patient outcomes. VR platform Osso VR is one example of a VR platform that's helping surgeons practise procedures before operating on patients. AR system AccuVein uses a handheld scanner to help nurses find patients' veins for blood draws and IV insertions. Brainlab, a mixed reality platform, assists surgeons in planning and performing minimally invasive surgeries.

In education, ER can create immersive learning environments that enable students to interact with complex concepts, bringing them to life in ways that traditional teaching methods can't. Nearpod, an interactive classroom platform, uses AR to allow students to explore and engage with virtual objects in the real world. VR system zSpace lets students and teachers interact with 3D models of objects in a variety of subjects, from anatomy to engineering. VR platform VictoryXR literally and metaphorically immerses students in subjects such as science, history and language.

In entertainment, ER can provide interactive experiences that blur the lines between reality and fiction, creating unforgettable memories for audiences. The Void is a VR entertainment centre that provides immersive VR experiences such as Star Wars: Secrets of the Empire and Ghostbusters: Dimension. VR company Dreamscape Immersive offers a range of experiences from underwater adventures to alien encounters. I've personally tried Zero Latency VR in Melbourne, a free-roam VR gaming experience that lets players explore digital environments with friends.

In manufacturing, Boeing uses AR systems to assist in the assembly of planes and other aircraft. Ford uses VR systems to design and test new cars and trucks before building physical prototypes. Thyssenkrupp, a German engineering firm, uses AR to train employees and provide remote support for maintenance and repair tasks.

There are endless potential applications of ER technology, and its impact on different industries can be transformative. By putting people first and designing technology around their needs and experiences, we can unlock the full potential of ER technology and create a better, more exciting world for everyone.

THERE ARE ENDLESS POTENTIAL APPLICATIONS OF ER TECHNOLOGY, AND ITS IMPACT ON DIFFERENT INDUSTRIES CAN BE TRANSFORMATIVE.

A balm for global crises

The COVID-19 pandemic showed us that social isolation and lone-liness can have a severe impact on mental and physical health. However, with the use of ER, we may be able to combat these issues during future pandemics.

VR and AR can create a sense of presence and connectedness, making it possible for people to participate in events and activities from the comfort and safety of their own homes. During the pandemic there were virtual meditation sessions, concerts and comedy nights that could be accessed through VR technology. People were able to connect with their loved ones and even make new connections through these virtual events. In future pandemics, this technology could be leveraged to combat loneliness and isolation, especially among the elderly who are at higher risk of social isolation.

Several friends of mine left Melbourne during and straight after the pandemic. Many people I know who still live there are suffering from social awkwardness, experiencing flashbacks and having difficulty recalibrating in the post-COVID world. Melbourne went from most livable to most locked-down city in the world. Can you imagine what the city and its residents would be like today if ER was used in the Victorian Government's pandemic response to combat feelings of loneliness and disconnection? We can only hypothesise.

Many studies have shown a positive correlation between social networks and life expectancy.[30] Research published in the journal *PLoS Medicine* found that social relationships have a significant impact on mortality risk. The study analysed data from 148 studies involving more than 300,000 participants and found that individuals with strong social connections had a 50 per cent increased likelihood of survival compared to those with weaker social connections.[31]

A study published in the *American Journal of Epidemiology* found that social isolation was associated with an increased risk of mortality.[32] The study followed more than 9,000 adults over the age of 65 for seven years and found that individuals who were socially isolated had a 26 per cent higher risk of death compared to those who were not.

A third study, published in *Health & Quality of Life Outcomes,* found that social support was associated with better health outcomes among individuals with chronic illness.

These studies show that social networks play an important role in promoting health and longevity, and that individuals with strong social connections may be better equipped to deal with life's challenges and stressors. Therefore, by using ER to enhance social networks, we could potentially help people live longer and healthier lives. With the ability to participate in virtual social events and activities, people may be able to maintain and even strengthen their social connections during a pandemic or other times in which their mobility is limited.

WITH THE POTENTIAL TO COMBAT LONELINESS AND ISOLATION, ER COULD HELP US LIVE LONGER AND HEALTHIER LIVES WHILE ALSO PROVIDING US WITH NEW WAYS TO CONNECT WITH ONE ANOTHER.

The COVID-19 pandemic forced us to rethink how we connect with each other, and ER technology may be a valuable tool in the future. With the potential to combat loneliness and isolation, ER could help us live longer and healthier lives while also providing us with new ways to connect with one another.

ER can also benefit people with disabilities. For example, someone with limited mobility could use ER technology to visit a virtual museum, travel the world, or attend events and concerts from the comfort of their home. This could significantly improve their quality of life and reduce feelings of isolation.

Game changers – the new era of interactive experiences

The rise of ER has undoubtedly influenced the gaming industry. As the global AR and VR market is expected to grow to US$451.5 billion by 2030, Millennials and Gen Zs are no strangers to the concept of ER.[33] In recent years we have seen a new generation of gamers who have grown up with – and, in some cases, become addicted to – the immersive first-person experiences. These gamers have been exposed to the idea of ER through games such as Fortnite, Minecraft and Roblox, which offer open virtual worlds for gamers to interact with. Gamers are no longer satisfied with the flat screens of the past; they want to walk in the game's environment and interact with the elements around them.

One of the biggest appeals of VR gaming is its high level of engagement and immersion, which creates an extraordinary experience for gamers. Technology has successfully created a virtual world that feels real, allowing gamers to feel like they are part of the game. This level of immersion is expected to continue to improve as ER technology advances.

As ER continues to develop, the gaming industry is likely to be at the forefront of its applications. It is possible that we will see more games that utilise ER technology, providing even more immersive experiences for gamers. The rise of gaming technology in the past few years has shown that gamers are looking for more than just entertainment; they want to be a part of the experience, and ER technology offers them that opportunity. Gamers are chasing the feeling that they are connected to something bigger than themselves.

PEOPLE UNDERESTIMATE THEIR CAPACITY FOR CHANGE. THERE IS NEVER A RIGHT TIME TO DO A DIFFICULT THING.

JOHN PORTER

But how does this relate to the working word? Well, it isn't only gamers who are hooked on the immersive experience of ER. Here's how some of the world's biggest organisations are leveraging VR to satisfy humans' natural inclination to play:

- Swedish automaker Volvo has incorporated VR technology into its car-buying experience by creating a virtual showroom. This allows customers to experience different models and configurations without having to physically visit a dealership.

- German airline Lufthansa has created a VR experience to showcase its business class cabins to potential customers. This allows customers to experience the luxurious features of the cabin before booking a flight.

- German multinational conglomerate Siemens uses VR to train employees and demonstrate its products to customers. It has created virtual simulations of its factories and products, allowing employees and customers to learn and interact in a safe, controlled environment.

> **PEOPLE CHANGE FOR TWO MAIN REASONS: EITHER THEIR MINDS HAVE BEEN OPENED OR THEIR HEARTS HAVE BEEN BROKEN.**
>
> STEVEN AITCHISON

- The British-Dutch oil and gas company Royal Dutch Shell uses VR to train employees in hazardous and high-risk situations. It has created a virtual environment to simulate emergency scenarios and gamified learning to respond to real-life dangerous situations.

- French automaker Renault has incorporated VR technology into its production process. It uses VR to simulate the assembly line process and test different configurations, allowing it to improve efficiency and reduce waste in their manufacturing process.

Accessibility, affordability and actualisation

Accessibility and affordability are crucial factors in the widespread adoption of ER technology. In the past, new technologies were often out of reach for most due to high prices, but this is changing rapidly. ER is now within reach of a large portion of the population, and its becoming more accessible. The recent appearance of low-cost VR technologies (such as the Oculus Rift, the HTC Vive and the Sony PlayStation VR), and mixed reality interfaces (MRITF; such as Microsoft's HoloLens) is attracting worldwide attention. This may be the next largest stepping stone in the affordability of technological innovation.

Air glass and AR glasses supporting touch, voice and head tracking are already on the market. When first launched, new technology usually has a high price point as organisations aim to recoup their R&D and product development costs. The first VR AR headsets were retailing at around US$3000 to $5000. Today, Oculus headsets retail at under US$500.

Case studies are real, relatable and there for the taking. Imagine flying to another country to deliver an important client presentation. From the moment you step off the plane, your smart glasses depict the fastest route to your destination, painting unobtrusive waypoints in your field of vision while keeping track of public transport and traffic updates via your smartphone. One app highlights the restaurants correlating with your dietary requirements, another translates conversations into your native language. You reach your client's offices with time to spare and sit in the lobby, centring yourself and going over your work one final time. When you walk into the room, you're ready to rock and roll. You grant access to those physically in the room, knowing they'll be able to see your prototype via their own glasses as you demonstrate its features. This technology is already a reality. Sign me up!

> ## INCREDIBLE CHANGE HAPPENS IN YOUR LIFE WHEN YOU DECIDE TO TAKE CONTROL OF WHAT YOU DO HAVE POWER OVER INSTEAD OF CRAVING CONTROL OVER WHAT YOU DON'T.
>
> ### STEVE MARABOLI

As ER becomes more affordable and accessible, its potential applications are vast. We are only scratching the surface of what this technology can achieve. To make the most of it, it is crucial to ensure that people have access to the tools and knowledge required to use ER effectively. Cyber gloves enable head, hand, voice and gesture control. With a flick of your wrist or simple gesturing of your fingers, you can live your best *Minority Report* life – your digits controlling all things digital, reaching in and manipulating floating images like an orchestra conductor. But if you don't know how to use these tools, your high-tech cyber gloves may as well be Elton John's bedazzled weight-lifting mitts. As the saying goes, 'the tool is only powerful if people use it'. It is essential to provide training and education to ensure that ER is used effectively and benefits as many people as possible.

ER HAS THE POTENTIAL TO REVOLUTIONISE THE WAY WE LIVE, WORK AND INTERACT WITH THE WORLD AROUND US FOR THE BETTER – IF WE USE IT EFFECTIVELY AND ETHICALLY.

As the cost of ER technologies continues to decrease, we can expect to see widespread adoption across many fields. ER has the potential to revolutionise the way we live, work and interact with the world around us for the better – if we use it effectively and ethically.

PAUSE AND REFLECT

- How might accessibility and inclusiveness unlock untapped potential in terms of productivity, cost savings and employee engagement in your business? Reflect on the ways in which removing barriers, accommodating diverse needs and fostering a culture of inclusiveness can lead to increased innovation, collaboration and overall organisational performance.

- What can you as an individual do to elevate accessibility and inclusiveness during organisational change?

- What are the benefits to organisations that prioritise accessibility and inclusiveness as part of their trans-formation journey? Explore strategies for integrating accessibility and inclusiveness into the organisational culture, policies, processes and physical spaces, and reflect on the importance of leadership commitment, stakeholder engagement and continuous improvement to ensure sustainable change. Consider the positive impacts on employee morale, retention, customer satisfaction, market reach and overall competitiveness, and reflect on how these factors can contribute to unlocking additional potential within the organisation.

CHAPTER 6

MINING FOR GOLD, MINING FOR CHANGE

I want to share a personal first-hand experience I had with AR when I was heading up change management for a large gold miner.

AR is a technology that superimposes a computer-generated image on a user's view of the real world, thus providing a composite view. It incorporates three features:

1. a combination of digital and physical worlds

2. interactions are made in real time

3. accurate 3D identification of virtual and real objects.

This technology is more common than you think. You may be using some AR apps without even knowing it: Snapchat, Google Lens and YouCam Makeup are apps in this category. Those silly filters that add googly cartoon eyes or give you bunny ears? Yep, that's AR.

Back to my gold mining example. AR was used as a training delivery approach for a high-risk role in the gold mining process. Gold mining is a lucrative, complex industry that is fraught with regulatory, health, environmental and safety risks. Gone are the days of manual extraction processes such as gold panning. Mines are getting deeper, bigger and more expensive to run. This means more advanced extraction techniques such as pit mining and gold cyanidation have come to the fore.

Some of these more advanced techniques need special machinery such as the autoclave. AR was used to conduct autoclave training. You may be wondering, what on earth is an autoclave? Well, it's not so much *on* earth; rather, mined earth containing gold goes *in* it.

The backdrop of transformation in mining

Enormous. Complex. Hot. Dangerous. The mining processes that occur in an autoclave are elaborate to explain.

Pressure oxidation is a process for extracting gold from refractory ore. Pyrite and arsenopyrite are common refractory ores that trap gold within them. Refractory ores require pretreatment before the gold can be adequately extracted.

The pressure oxidation process is used to prepare such ores for conventional gold extraction processes such as cyanidation. It is performed in an autoclave at high pressure and temperature, where high-purity oxygen mixes with a slurry of ore. When the original sulfide minerals are oxidised at high temperature and pressure the trapped gold is released. Pressure oxidation has a very high gold recovery rate – normally at least 10 per cent higher than roasting.

In simple terms, think of a four-storey oven that bakes precious metals instead of cookies, at temperatures and pressures more intense than anything found naturally in the atmosphere. It's a dangerous piece of equipment even if you know what you're doing with it.

On Lihir Island in Papua New Guinea (PNG), 700 kilometres north-east of Port Moresby, AR overlays of the autoclave were created. The gold deposit at Lihir is within the Luise caldera, an extinct volcanic crater that is geothermally active. It's one of the largest known gold deposits in the world.

This is not the typical work environment you might think of. Remnant geothermal activity is present in the Luise caldera, as evidenced by hot springs and fumaroles. The mine site experiences 90 per cent humidity with temperatures averaging 32 degrees Celsius. It looks like the love child of *Avatar* and *Jurassic Park* – chirping birds, lush tropical jungles, indigenous tribespeople – minus the blue aliens and dinosaurs.

THE FUTURE FIT ORGANISATION

From high country to high tech

Close to 95 per cent of the workforce at the mine are local PNG nationals. Many leave their remote mountain tribes to work in mining. Mining has dominated the PNG economy since the 1970s. With the exception of the Ok Tedi Mine (copper-gold) almost all of the mining in PNG has been gold mining. The two largest gold mines are the Porgera (Enga Province) and Lihir (New Ireland Province) mines. Needless to say, mining is a big employer in the country.

PNG is not only rich in resources, but in indigenous culture. Among the country's population of 9 million people, more than 850 languages are spoken and there are more than 600 distinct tribes. Because many tribes were cut off from each other – as well as the outside world – for hundreds of years, cultures and traditions vary greatly from region to region. Many indigenous peoples don their traditional costumes and perform their ritual dances at PNG's famous cultural festivals. But while the presence of these tribes at festivals – known as sing-sings – means we know more than ever about them, many of their customs and traditions remain shrouded in mystery. It really is like being transported back to the land that time forgot.

The tribe residing in PNG's Highland region is known for its skeleton dance, and for wearing headdresses made of moss and soil. The Baining people are also famous for their fire dance. Young women receive tattoos as a rite of passage and a sign that they are ready for marriage. The tattoos are given to them between the ages of 14 and 18; they are created by female elders, who pierce the skin with a thorn and dye the cuts with a mix of charcoal and water. These tattoos resemble crocodile skin, which is considered a symbol of strength and power in the province. On the other hand, young men in

> SOME CHANGES LOOK NEGATIVE ON THE SURFACE BUT YOU WILL SOON REALIZE THAT SPACE IS BEING CREATED IN YOUR LIFE FOR SOMETHING NEW TO EMERGE.
>
> ECKHART TOLLE

the Sepik region go through a difficult initiation ceremony that marks their skin on their backs and shoulders. These practices have been passed down through generations.

With so much diversity present in the people being trained, the organisation needed a way to help galvanise everyone into one shared experience. Enter VR.

The future of training

Advancements in technology have revolutionised the way we approach training, especially when it comes to high-risk environments such as mining sites. With the help of ER solutions, companies are now able to provide their employees with a safer and more immersive learning experience.

The use of ER in hazardous training environments has had a significant impact on how these industries operate. In the past, training was conducted by a single person, which often created a bottleneck effect when that person was unavailable. This resulted in delays and potential risks to the trainees, as they were unable to receive the necessary training and information in a timely manner. However, with the introduction of ER, these risks have been significantly reduced, as the need for a human trainer in a potentially hazardous environment has been eliminated.

One example of the application of ER in hazardous training is the autoclave at a mining site. As I mentioned, the autoclave is a piece of equipment that poses a significant safety risk to both instructors and trainees. It reaches high temperatures of up to 240 degrees Celsius. By leveraging ER technology, trainees can now simulate working with the autoclave in a virtual environment, reducing the risks associated with training using the actual machine.

ER solutions have also made training more engaging and effective. With the ability to create a 4D immersive environment, trainees can walk into hypothetical situations and apply their knowledge in a more practical way. This not only makes the training process more engaging, but it also helps trainees retain the information more effectively.

ADVANCEMENTS IN TECHNOLOGY HAVE REVOLUTIONISED TRAINING, ESPECIALLY THOSE IN HIGH-RISK ENVIRONMENTS.

In addition to providing a safer and more immersive learning experience, ER solutions have also helped reduce training costs. With the elimination of the human trainer in potentially hazardous environments, companies can save on the costs associated with hiring and training instructors, as well as the costs of providing safety equipment and protective gear.

By providing a safer, more immersive and cost-effective training experience, ER solutions have become an essential tool for preparing employees for high-risk environments. As technology continues to advance, we can expect to see even more innovative uses of ER in the training and development of employees across a wide range of industries – not just the dangerous ones.

Induction training reimagined

I've worked for many large organisations where induction training was conducted completely online. Watching cartoon videos on ethics, governance and compliance then being asked insanely boring questions about what I just watched is not my idea of fun. In fact, it's so not my idea of fun that I'll admit I have pressed the fast forward button and guessed the right answer. Most of the time, I guessed correctly.

Now imagine if these scenarios were in 4D, where I could walk into a hypothetical situation and determine the appropriate course of action by acting it out? Now that's interesting. That's the future of training.

WHEN IT COMES TO TRAINING, SOME COMPANIES ARE MORE FUTURE-FORWARD THAN OTHERS.

When it comes to training, some companies are more future-forward than others. Here are some examples of those on the front foot:

- Walmart has implemented VR training for its employees. The program, called Walmart Academy, uses VR headsets to simulate real-world scenarios and provide employees with hands-on experience in various roles.

- H&M created a mobile app called Welcome to H&M that provides new hires with an interactive, gamified training experience. The app includes quizzes, videos and interactive scenarios to help employees learn about the company's culture and policies.

- KFC created a virtual escape room game as part of its employee training program. The game challenges employees to solve puzzles and answer questions related to food safety and customer service.

- McDonald's has used a mobile game app called McGame to train new employees on kitchen and service procedures. The app includes inter-active games and quizzes to help employees learn about the company's processes and policies.

- Marriott International has implemented a training program called M Live Studios, using VR and AR to simulate customer interactions and provide employees with hands-on training in various roles, such as front desk and housekeeping.

Where does your organisation sit on the future fit training spectrum?

Beam me up, Scotty!

You've probably guessed by now that I'm a big believer in experiencing anything and everything for myself. I had to try the AR training program for the autoclave machine.

I donned the Oculus headset. I remember it was the middle of winter – one of those cold and miserable Melbourne days. I was wearing not just one, but *two* pairs of tights, and my trusty black puffer jacket.

It was surreal.

Experiencing the training felt like I was *actually* there – high up in the air, walking along the suspended steel beams. I saw the instructor so clearly in front of me, espousing the machine's technical specifications. The sun was shining and I narrowed my eyes and squinted.

I forgot all about the headset and that I was bundled up like an Eskimo. My brain knew it was impossible, but I swear I actually *felt* the island heat on my face.

Because of the experiential nature of the training, the trainee operators retained *35 per cent* more information post-training compared to when they received in-person training delivered by a human. Safety and productivity improved because of their familiarity with the site and the autoclave before even setting foot in it.

The upside of leveraging AR training for the autoclave machine in PNG was tremendous. The technology provided an immersive and engaging learning experience. However, the success of the technology depended on its adoption.

To achieve this, the team had to design the technology around the needs, wants and traits of the operators – the people stack. Safety was a top priority, so the training had to be safe. Convenience and accessibility were also critical, so the team had to reduce the fear of the unknown associated with new technology and make the AR experience even richer than the physical world to produce a spike in excitement and curiosity.

But despite the success of the AR pilot the initiative did not go any further.

Even though this technology could be scaled or replicated to train people in other high-risk roles, or be integrated into other training programs or processes, the lack of continued focus and investment in the people stack meant it was impossible to drive more innovation and push through expected resistance and whet the appetite for more change.

The lesson here is clear: the success of any technological innovation depends on the people who use it, the leaders who back it and the influencers who advocate for it. The team's investment in the people stack was critical to the success of the AR training, and it would be equally critical to any future technological innovation. Without investing in people, the next quantum leap forward will never happen, and the potential benefits of technological innovations will not be fully realised. Investing in people must be a priority for any organisation seeking to successfully drive true digital transformation.

People stack fell flat

The story of the technology that went underutilised despite its potential highlights a crucial aspect of successful digital transformation: investing in people. As organisations race to adopt new technologies and drive innovation, it's easy to focus solely on technological advancements and forget that the people who will be using those tools are equally, if not more, important.

Resistance to change is a common and expected hurdle in successful digital transformation. While technology can make work easier and safer, it's only effective if people embrace it and use it. Investments in people is critical to drive behaviour change and ensure that the organisation can leverage new technology to its full potential. This investment can take many forms, including on-the-job training, upskilling and reskilling programs.

However, investing in people goes beyond just training them to use new technology. It also means creating a culture that fosters innovation, risk-taking and continuous learning. Leaders need to prioritise

> # AND THAT IS HOW CHANGE HAPPENS. ONE GESTURE. ONE PERSON. ONE MOMENT AT A TIME.
> ## LIBBA BRAY

employee engagement, wellbeing and career development to drive innovation and progress. They must also be transparent and communicate the benefits and objectives of digital transformation to employees, so they understand how their work fits into the bigger picture.

Ignoring the people stack and focusing solely on technology is a recipe for failure. There have been too many instances in the corporate graveyard where the needs and perspectives of employees were ignored, with disastrous results. One example is the case of FoxMeyer Drug, a pharmaceutical wholesaler that filed for bankruptcy in 1996 after the failed implementation of a $100 million enterprise resource planning (ERP) system. The company's management had focused solely on the technological aspects of the implementation, neglecting to involve employees in the process and failing to address concerns regarding the compatibility of the new system with existing business processes. The change wasn't adopted, with the new system leading to significant operational disruptions, order processing delays and lost revenue.

Another example is the UK National Health Service's (NHS) implementation of a new electronic patient record system in 2011. The system was designed to provide a unified platform for patient data management across different hospitals and care facilities. However, the implementation failed due to underinvestment in user adoption and training. The system was not user-friendly and didn't address the specific needs of different medical professionals. As a result, many doctors and nurses – the key users of the system – found it challenging to use, leading to operational inefficiencies and errors in patient care.

In both cases, ignoring the people involved and focusing solely on the technology led to significant negative impacts on operations, and the reputations of both the company and the leadership team. Organisations must prioritise the needs and perspectives of their employees and involve them in the implementation process, co-creating the change strategy side by side, to ensure successful adoption of new technology.

Leaders must understand that technological innovations alone will not drive progress; they need to prioritise investing in their people to get the benefits of new technology. By doing so, they can create a culture of innovation to drive success in the long run.

> **LEADERS MUST UNDERSTAND THAT TECHNOLOGICAL INNOVATIONS ALONE WILL NOT DRIVE PROGRESS.**

PAUSE AND REFLECT

- How can you cultivate a culture of continuous learning in your team/department/organisation? Reflect on the importance of embracing a growth mindset, providing learning opportunities, fostering knowledge sharing and creating an environment that values curiosity, experimentation and ongoing development.

- What emerging trends and technologies hold the potential to revolutionise learning in your organisation? Consider advancements in AI, VR, personalised learning platforms, microlearning and other innovative approaches that can enhance the effectiveness, accessibility and scalability of learning initiatives.

- How do you learn best? What about your team members? How can you bridge the gap between formal and informal learning to create a holistic learning ecosystem? Reflect on the integration of formal training programs, on-the-job learning experiences, mentorship, social learning platforms and other strategies that facilitate continuous learning and knowledge transfer across the organisation.

CHAPTER 7

EXPERIENCE THE EXTRAORDINARY

People often ask me how I became adept at helping others accept and embrace the new and foreign. It's not rocket science: I often literally and metaphorically walk a mile in their shoes.

After the most basic human needs of shelter, food and physical safety are met, at the end of the day we just want to be heard.

When we feel heard, we feel seen. When we feel seen, we feel accepted. When we feel accepted, we lower our defenses.

You may know demonstrating empathy is positive for people, but new research demonstrates its importance for everything from innovation to retention.[34] Great leadership requires a heady mix of all kinds of skills to create the conditions for engagement, happiness and performance, and empathy tops the list of what leaders must get right.

> WHEN WE FEEL HEARD, WE FEEL SEEN. WHEN WE FEEL SEEN, WE FEEL ACCEPTED. WHEN WE FEEL ACCEPTED, WE LOWER OUR DEFENSES.

Empathy is a critical skill for leaders to develop and demonstrate in the workplace. It's not just about being nice or compassionate; empathy drives positive relationships, organisational culture and business results. The ability to consider someone else's thoughts and feelings is essential for building trust, fostering creativity and innovation and retaining top talent.

The 2019 Businessolver State of Workplace Empathy report found that 93 per cent of employees would stay with an empathetic employer.[35] Furthermore, 82 per cent of employees said they would be more likely to stay with a company that shows empathy, while 60 per cent of employees said they would take a pay cut to work for an empathetic employer. Therefore, empathy isn't just important for employees; it's crucial for business success.

> **THE ONLY WAY TO MAKE SENSE OUT OF CHANGE IS TO PLUNGE INTO IT, MOVE WITH IT, AND JOIN THE DANCE.**
>
> **ALAN WATTS**

Empathy contributes to positive relationships and organisational cultures and it also drives results. Empathy may not be a brand-new skill, but it has a new level of importance; the latest research makes it especially clear that empathy is the leadership competency to develop and demonstrate now and in the future.

How to demonstrate empathy

Leaders can demonstrate empathy in two ways.

First, they can consider someone else's thoughts through cognitive empathy ('If I were in their position, what would I be thinking right now?'). This approach requires leaders to consider what they would think and feel if they were in the other person's situation.

Cognitive empathy

Cognitive empathy is when you imagine what it might be like to be that person – where you 'walk a mile in their shoes' to better understand their lived experience. Imagine your friend doesn't win an award they've been nominated for. You know they are hurt and disappointed, and you understand why they would feel this way after getting excited about their nomination and working so hard on their achievements. This is cognitive empathy because you're imagining what it's like being that person during that moment. This is different from looking at the situation from our own perspective, such as by remembering that the person is talented and may win the award next year.

Second, leaders can focus on a person's feelings using emotional empathy ('Being in their position would make me feel . . .'). This involves recognising and acknowledging others' emotions and showing compassion and understanding towards them.

EXAMPLE IS NOT THE MAIN THING IN INFLUENCING OTHERS. IT IS THE ONLY THING.

ALBERT SCHWEITZER

Emotional empathy

Emotional empathy is when you literally feel another person's emotions. If you're sitting close to a loved one and they start to cry because of the recent passing of a friend, you might begin to feel sad too. What they are experiencing emotionally has an impact on your own emotional state.

Leaders will be most successful when they not only personally consider others, but when they express their concerns and inquire about challenges directly, and then listen to employees' responses.

Leaders don't have to be experts in mental health to demonstrate they care and are paying attention. It's enough to check in, ask questions and take cues from the employee about how much they want to share.

To be most effective, leaders should combine cognitive and emotional empathy and express their concerns directly to employees while listening to their responses. Active listening is an essential component of empathy. When leaders listen carefully to employees, they can gain a better understanding of their needs and concerns, which can help them address those concerns and build stronger relationships.

> **EVERYONE THINKS OF CHANGING THE WORLD, BUT NO ONE THINKS OF CHANGING HIMSELF.**
>
> **LEO TOLSTOY**

Leaders who are struggling with empathy can begin by practising active listening, asking open-ended questions and showing genuine interest in what their employees have to say. Leaders should also strive to create a culture of empathy in their organisations. This means encouraging employees to show empathy to one another, recognising and rewarding empathetic behaviour, and promoting open communication.

Empathy is a crucial leadership competency to develop and demonstrate. It contributes to positive relationships, drives results and is essential for retaining top talent. Leaders who can demonstrate empathy will be more successful in creating engaged, happy and high-performing teams.

Blue lights, getting it right

When I was leading change management for a mission-critical technology implementation at the Western Australia Police Force, I had to get the whole 'blue lights' experience.

This meant riding in the back of a police wagon. It meant going out on the boats with the water police. It meant visiting the police horse stables and seeing how mounted officers interacted and stored technology while on patrol. It meant going to the shooting range, the cadets training academy, and 'walking the beat' with the officers on a hot summer night in a red light district.

In some calls we attended, I found myself shaking my head in disbelief that certain disputes and crimes were happening in my backyard. I'd seen some things in the news, such as cars being bombed, looting and families of eight living in one small room, but they were always in far-flung countries.

The things I saw have stayed with me – for good and bad.

The most important part of the experience was that I learned first-hand about the forces for and against adoption of the critical technology. By engaging and empathising with the employee end users I discovered opportunities to increase acceptance by tweaking and adjusting how we communicated, engaged and implemented the solution.

PEOPLE CANNOT CHANGE THE TRUTH BUT THE TRUTH CAN CHANGE PEOPLE.

UNKNOWN

You can't do this from the other end of a video call. Benjamin Franklin was spot on when he said, 'Tell me and I forget, teach me and I may remember, involve me and I learn.'

Most people would be unaware that the Western Australia Police Force is the single largest jurisdiction in the world. From remote communities to a thriving metropolitan city, its 6500 police officers preserve community safety across 2.5 million square kilometres.

THE MOST EFFECTIVE LEADERS ARE HUMBLE ENOUGH TO REALISE THOSE SUPPORTING THEM FROM BELOW NEED TO BE TAKEN CARE OF FIRST.

Leading such a geographically dispersed and diversely skilled team (including bomb experts, TRG, K9, mounted police, forensics, air wing and water police, to name a few) requires incredible leadership prowess. These leaders don't have the luxury of offering hefty bonuses or work-place perks to motivate and influence employees.

I'd like to share some of the takeaways I learned about change and leadership from the exceptional people I worked with at this organisation.

It's not about the top of the pyramid, but the bottom

Too often, there's a disproportionate focus on managing up. The most effective leaders are humble enough to realise those supporting them from below need to be taken care of first. These leaders remove obstacles and provide tools and resources to set their team up for success. This boosts employee morale, increases capability and enhances self-esteem. Oh, and in case you missed it, it also supports achieving the 'bigger picture'.

> A LEADER TAKES PEOPLE WHERE THEY WANT TO GO. A GREAT LEADER TAKES PEOPLE WHERE THEY DON'T NECESSARILY WANT TO GO, BUT OUGHT TO BE.
>
> ROSALYNN CARTER

You can't lead without passion

The best leaders I worked with at the Western Australia Police Force were those who love their industry, their job and all that it stands for – not just the leading part. The most enthusiastic leaders have a cult-like following. Their energy is contagious. Regardless of how they arrived at their current role, whether it was working their way up as a fresh-faced cadet or graduating from the academy as a late starter, their work ethic and authenticity is undeniable. They prove themselves quickly, cementing their reputation as a credible force to be reckoned with.

Leadership should be hands-on and visible

The greatest leaders are never closed off in their office – they exert significant effort to understand the organisation, its people, its challenges and the potential opportunities they may be able to harvest. The most hands-on leaders understand not only the roles and responsibilities of each department, but the dependencies and underlying political landscape it operates in. Visibility breeds trust – critical to gaining support for massive change.

Communication and stakeholder engagement are paramount

The most effective leaders know most changes will not be received with open arms, or even a hint of a smile. Their response? Communication, involvement and education. Employees don't have to love every decision that's made, but they sure need to understand the rationale driving it. By involving impacted stakeholders early, leaders are able to facilitate understanding of the 'why' which eventually morphs into (at times begrudging) acceptance. This mitigates covert cynicism and ingrained resistance, which can be fatal to a change initiative.

> **TO HANDLE YOURSELF, USE YOUR HEAD; TO HANDLE OTHERS, USE YOUR HEART.**
>
> **ELEANOR ROOSEVELT**

Accessibility and responsiveness are key

I reported directly to a high-ranking Western Australia officer who is a natural leader and gifted communicator. He understands the importance of communicating with all stakeholders, especially employees, and hosts regular presentations and demonstrations to hear employee concerns and feedback first-hand. His door is always open and questions are encouraged from everyone. Oh, and he's an email fiend. If you email him directly, you'll likely have a response within 24 hours. His quick and personal response demonstrates he values the input of others.

We all love story time

The art of storytelling is a potent tool. Most of us were read stories during our childhood, or can recount a favourite fable. Stories stick in our memory. The most effective leaders share their own 'war stories' to connect more personally with employees. The message is powerful, and the story approach explains corporate decisions much more effectively than any glossy business case could.

Connectivity and teamwork are vital

Ideally every member of a team would work in the same office. In reality, teams are usually scattered in silos in disparate locations around the globe. The response to this is a working group with representatives who meet regularly – whether it be via video call or face to face. This facilitates understanding of each party's role, enables learning from one another's insights and reminds everyone of the bigger picture. These recurring meetings were instituted and mandated early on in the Western Australia Police Force change project, and were effective not only in ensuring milestones were met, but in finding common ground – which developed strong social ties within the group.

Be a fly on the wall

Leaders most in touch with the 'pulse' of the organisation have sharply honed observation skills. My 'ride along' with one of the police units helped me understand the significance, pain points and desired future state of the new technology I was engaged to implement. I encourage you to sit for an hour and just observe: whether it's in the lobby, work area or meeting hub. I guarantee you'll come back with ideas to improve processes or the client experience.

NOT ONLY DO GREAT LEADERS HOLD PEOPLE ACCOUNTABLE, THEY HOLD THEMSELVES UP TO THE SAME STANDARD.

Playing nice only gets you so far

Not only do great leaders hold people accountable, they hold themselves up to the same standard. I've seen leaders 'fall on their sword' by acknowledging the impact of their actions (or inaction). They then communicate their next steps or propose a solution. There's no buck passing or mutterings such as 'I couldn't have seen it coming.' This approach commands respect and instills confidence that history won't repeat itself.

These lessons aren't new. What is rare, though, is someone who embraces them, applies them and lives by them. Change is hard to implement; especially when you're shaking up an ingrained mindset that fiercely guards its authoritative structure. It necessitates detailed introspection, enhanced emotional intelligence and the influence to convince others to share – and support – your vision. But most of all, it requires a leader to step forward.

The leaders I encountered at the Western Australian Police Force were on par with the foresight, astuteness, and willingness to adapt as those in the most innovative and successful businesses in the private sector. If teamwork, passion and communication are some of the key ingredients to success, leadership is the method that brings it all together.

PAUSE AND REFLECT

- How do your leadership actions during times of change impact the overall success of the transformation? Reflect on the ways in which your leadership style, communication and decision-making influence employee engagement, resilience and willingness to embrace change.

- In what ways do you effectively lead by example and inspire others during times of change? Consider how your own attitudes, mindset and actions can serve as a source of motivation, trust and stability for your team. Reflect on strategies to demonstrate authenticity, empathy and resilience in navigating the complexities of change.

- How can you leverage your leadership role to empower and support individuals and teams throughout the change process? Reflect on the importance of providing clarity, resources and opportunities for growth, as well as fostering a culture of psychological safety, collaboration and continuous learning, to enable individuals and teams to thrive amid change.

CHAPTER 8

WE'RE ALL CHIEF MINDSET OFFICERS

Remember the two transformative traits I hunt for when building my A+ transformation team? Openness to change and assuming positive intent.

During my time at the large mining company, I found those two transformative traits were lacking. We only had a few golden moments before the lights were dimmed.

When I reflect on my experience there, one thing stands out to me: the importance of mindset.

When it comes to driving digital transformation, mindset plays a critical role in success. As the old saying goes, 'Change starts from within.' As a leader it's essential to have an open and positive attitude when undertaking any transformation effort, as this sets the tone for the entire organisation.

At the mining company, people were hesitant to embrace change. They clung to their old habits and routines, reluctant to try new things or explore uncharted territories. It made the transformation effort much harder, and progress was glacially slow.

But it wasn't just about being open to change. It was also about assuming positive intent. If people assume positive intent, this creates a culture of collaboration and openness, where people are willing to work together towards a common goal. Too often people assume the worst-case scenario or think that others are out to get them. This leads to a culture of mistrust, which is detrimental to any transformation effort. In the case of the mining company, it made it extremely difficult to explore the unknown, push through resistance or combat unspoken fears. As a result, the transformation effort at the biggest gold miner in the southern hemisphere ground to a halt.

I believe digital transformation is a lot like a romantic partnership. Just like a successful relationship requires each person to be open to change, digital transformation requires employees to be open to new ideas and approaches. In a romantic partnership, assuming positive intent leads to better outcomes, just like in a transformation effort. Both require people to be open to changing themselves and their habits or routines to benefit the greater good. In a good relationship, one partner leaving the toilet seat up is seen as a forgetful mistake rather than a deliberate attempt to make the other person's life miserable. Adopting this mindset leads to better outcomes.

JUST LIKE A SUCCESSFUL RELATIONSHIP REQUIRES EACH PERSON TO BE OPEN TO CHANGE, DIGITAL TRANSFORMATION REQUIRES EMPLOYEES TO BE OPEN TO NEW IDEAS AND APPROACHES.

Mindset is critical when it comes to driving change. It highlights the importance of suspending judgement even in the face of resistance or uncertainty. It underscores that those who embrace change are those who will come out on top, while those who resist will be left behind. Ultimately, the key to driving progress and innovation is all about how your mind views change. It's about seeing change as an opportunity rather than a threat, and understanding that growth requires you to step out of your comfort zone.

Mindset is critical. Having an open and positive attitude, assuming positive intent, and embracing innovation are all essential elements of a successful transformation effort. By creating a culture that embraces these traits, organisations can change before they have to while they continue to deliver value to their customers. In contrast, assuming negative intent leads to a culture of fear and mistrust, where people are hesitant to share ideas or take risks. This stifles innovation and progress, leading to a stagnant organisation that struggles to keep up with the times.

Some organisations live and breathe the concept of 'mind over matter'. Adidas is a German multinational corporation that has made a significant investment in digital transformation. The company prioritised mindset by creating a culture of innovation and experimentation. In 2017, Adidas launched a digital transformation program to enhance its e-commerce platform and optimise its supply chain. The company also created an innovation lab to develop new ideas, such as smart apparel and personalised products. It has created a strong digital presence – even stronger than its retail presence – to improve customer experience and drive revenue.

British-Dutch multinational consumer goods company Unilever has made a significant investment in digital transformation. It created the Unilever Compass, which aimed to create a culture of purpose-driven innovation. It identified three key behaviours that it wanted its employees to embody: 'be brave', 'experiment and learn' and 'collaborate to win'. Unilever also invested in upskilling its employees, providing training in areas such as sustainability and digital marketing. This approach resulted in increased innovation, with Unilever launching new products such as vegan ice cream and partnering with startups to develop new solutions.

> **THE GOOD AND BAD THINGS ARE WHAT FORM US AS PEOPLE . . . CHANGE MAKES US GROW.**
>
> **KATE WINSLET**

AXA, an insurance company headquartered in France, created AXA University. The program aimed to upskill employees in areas such as digital literacy, data analytics and cybersecurity. AXA also created a culture that encouraged experimentation and collaboration, where employees were supported to share ideas and work together to solve problems. This approach resulted in AXA launching new products such as on-demand insurance.

Mindset matters

Technological advancement is moving at an unprecedented rate, and businesses that fail to keep up are doomed to fall behind. But it's not just about investing in new technology – it's about embracing change, adopting a mindset that encourages innovation and ensuring your people are getting the most out of the tools and technology you have, as well as any new tech you introduce.

Think again of your granny driving a Ferrari. Having the latest and greatest tools at your disposal means nothing if you don't know how to use them. Granny will be shifting those tectonic

> **HAVING THE LATEST AND GREATEST TOOLS AT YOUR DISPOSAL MEANS NOTHING IF YOU DON'T KNOW HOW TO USE THEM.**

gears at the pace of tectonic plates coming together; toddling down the Autobahn like it's a school zone.

So much potential is never realised. Remember TomTom location mapping? What would have happened if TomTom partnered with taxi companies prior to Uber disrupting the industry? Do you think there'd be a need for Uber? Maybe not. All those years ago, capabilities such as location tracking, Garmin maps and Google already existed.

The failure of taxi companies to partner with TomTom is a prime example of what can happen when businesses become complacent and fail to innovate or see the value in available technology. The technology existed, yet the taxi industry chose to ignore it, assuming it was too big to fail. But as we all know, that's not what happened; and now traditional taxi companies are scrambling to catch up.

Why didn't taxi companies embrace innovation? Why didn't they future proof their business by adding TomTom into their tech stack? One word: mindset.

They were comfortable, complacent and cashed up, and they failed to embrace change. They regarded themselves as too much of a protected species to put themselves in the customer's shoes and God forbid, take proactive action to improve customer experience. And it all comes down to mindset – the willingness to embrace change, try new things, and put the customer first.

The lesson here is clear: in today's rapidly evolving business land-scape, companies that don't innovate will be left behind. It's not enough to simply invest in new technology – you need to be willing to change your entire mindset and way of doing things. Those who constantly push the boundaries and look for ways to innovate and improve are those who will win. The pace of technological advance-ment isn't slowing down any time soon, so the only way to succeed is to keep up.

German logistics company DB Schenker has done a lot of work on its future fitness capabilities, undergoing a significant digital transfor-mation in recent years. The company launched Digital Mindset, an initiative to encourage its employees to adopt a digital-first mindset and to embrace technology to drive business success. Digital Mindset involved a range of activities including workshops, training sessions and digital coaching to help employees at all levels understand the benefits of digital transformation, and develop the skills and confi-dence needed to leverage new technologies.

As a result of this initiative, DB Schenker was able to drive signifi-cant improvements in its operations and customer experience. The company launched a range of new digital services, including a mobile app for tracking shipments, and implemented new technologies such as drones and robotics in its warehouses. In addition, DB Schenker was able to significantly reduce its costs and increase efficiency, leading to improved financial performance.

Over-indexing on tech tools

If your organisation over-indexes on technology, the initial benefits may seem sweet but will likely prove to be short-lived. The truth is, technology alone will not drive long-term success. Digital transformation requires more than simply purchasing and implementing the latest and greatest tools.

Many organisations fall into the trap of over-indexing on technology because it's seen as the easiest and most straightforward solution. They believe that investing in technology will automatically result in improved efficiencies, increased profits and happier customers. But this conventional thinking is shortsighted and ignores the bigger picture.

Digital transformation is not just about technology; it's about fundamentally changing the way an organisation operates. It involves adopting a new mindset, culture and way of working that prioritises agility, flexibility and innovation. It's about creating an environment where employees are empowered to think creatively and take risks, and where failure is seen as an opportunity to learn and improve.

Here are some examples of how this plays out:

- Lego went through a digital and cultural transformation to stay relevant in the digital age. It shifted its focus from traditional toys to digital play experiences, introduced new digital products and apps and created a culture of innovation and experimentation.

- Technology company Philips transformed its culture to become more agile, customer-centric and innovative. It implemented new ways of working, such as design thinking and lean startup methodologies, and created a culture of experimentation and collaboration.

- Hospitality company Accor transformed its culture and operations to become more customer-centric, innovative and agile. It implemented new digital platforms and technologies, such as cloud computing and data analytics, and created a culture of experimentation and empowerment.

Over-indexing on technology hinders the process of digital transformation. When you focus solely on technology, you overlook the critical need for cultural and operational change. You may also fail to engage your employees in the transformation process, which can lead to resistance and, ultimately, failure.

To avoid falling into the trap of over-indexing on technology, you should start by assessing your current culture and operations. Identify areas where change is needed and involve employees in the process of designing and implementing solutions. This will help create a sense of ownership and accountability among employees.

Organisations must be willing to experiment and take calculated risks. They should not be afraid to try new things, even if they may fail. Failure is a natural part of the transformation process, and it's important to view it as an opportunity to grow.

FOR WHAT IT'S WORTH: IT'S NEVER TOO LATE OR, IN MY CASE, TOO EARLY TO BE WHOEVER YOU WANT TO BE. THERE'S NO TIME LIMIT; STOP WHENEVER YOU WANT. YOU CAN CHANGE OR STAY THE SAME, THERE ARE NO RULES TO THIS THING. WE CAN MAKE THE BEST OR THE WORST OF IT.

ERIC ROTH

> **AT LEAST 40 PER CENT OF ALL BUSINESSES WILL DIE IN THE NEXT 10 YEARS . . . IF THEY DON'T FIGURE OUT HOW TO CHANGE THEIR ENTIRE COMPANY TO ACCOMMODATE NEW TECHNOLOGIES.**
>
> JOHN CHAMBERS

Finally, a culture of continuous improvement should be prioritised. Digital transformation is not a one-time event but an ongoing journey. By continuously assessing and improving processes and operations, organisations can ensure they remain competitive in an ever-evolving digital landscape. Over-indexing on technology may provide some initial benefits, but it's not a sustainable solution for digital transformation. To truly transform, you must focus on cultural and operational change, engage your people, take risks, and prioritise continuous improvement.

Conventional thinking leads to conventional performance

Conventional thinking is the enemy of innovation and progress. It promotes a narrow and static view of the world, where the status quo is guarded ferociously and change is resisted. This kind of thinking is deeply ingrained in many industries and it can be difficult to break free from. But to stay profitable and relevant, businesses *must* challenge conventional thinking and embrace new perspectives.

One way to do this is by focusing on the people stack. This means looking beyond just the tools and technology that a business uses and considering the human element. Businesses must gain a deeper understanding of their users, people and customers and how they interact with technology. You can do this by asking questions such as 'What does a day in these people's lives look like?' and 'Which situations will this technology make life simpler, easier, more efficient or maybe even more fun?'

BUSINESSES MUST GAIN A DEEPER UNDERSTANDING OF THEIR USERS AND HOW THEY INTERACT WITH TECHNOLOGY.

This approach can lead to more solutions that are tailored to users' needs. Instead of just implementing the latest technology for the sake of it, focus on creating tools and experiences that truly add value to people's lives. This can result in more engaged and satisfied customers, as well as a more productive and motivated workforce.

However, breaking free from conventional thinking is not easy. It requires a willingness to challenge assumptions, take risks and think outside the box. It also requires a culture where failure is viewed as a necessary step on the path to success.

Not sure how to start? Here are a few ways:

- **Challenge assumptions:** One way to start thinking unconventionally is by questioning assumptions. Don't take things at face value. Challenge the status quo. Ask why things are done a certain way and consider alternative approaches.

- **Look for inspiration outside your industry:** Take inspiration from other industries and fields. Look for innovative ideas and practices outside of your industry and consider how they might be applied in your own work.

- **Experiment and iterate:** Don't be afraid to experiment and try new things. Embrace failure as a learning opportunity and use feedback to iterate and improve your ideas. By testing and refining new approaches, you can find innovative solutions that challenge conventional thinking.

There are plenty of organisations that are known for their outside-the-box thinking. Tesla, led by Elon Musk (love him or lump him), is known for being unconventional in its approach to the automotive industry. From electric cars to autonomous driving, Tesla has disrupted the traditional auto industry; this ethos is also permeating into X (formerly known as Twitter) now that Musk owns it.

Google, one of the world's largest technology companies, is also known for being unconventional. From its 20 per cent time policy – which allows employees to spend 20 per cent of their work time on projects of their own choosing – to its emphasis on data-driven decision-making, Google has disrupted the traditional approach to technology and business.

Outdoor clothing and gear company Patagonia also belongs in this camp. From donating 1 per cent of its sales to environmental causes to using recycled materials in its products, Patagonia has challenged traditional business practices and shown that profitability and sustainability can go hand in hand.

THE BIGGEST PART OF OUR DIGITAL TRANSFORMATION IS CHANGING THE WAY WE THINK.

SIMEON PRESTON

Ultimately, the dangers of conventional thinking are clear. Businesses that cling to outdated models and ways of thinking risk being left behind. By embracing a people-centric approach and challenging the norm, you can stay ahead of the curve and thrive in the face of uncertainty and change.

PAUSE AND REFLECT

- How does your mindset influence the way you approach and navigate organisational transformation? Reflect on your beliefs, attitudes and perceptions about change, and consider how they shape your decision-making, problem-solving and willingness to embrace new ideas and possibilities.

- What mindset shifts are necessary to foster a culture of innovation, adaptability and resilience within your team? Reflect on the importance of cultivating a growth mindset, embracing ambiguity and uncertainty, promoting a learning culture, and challenging limiting beliefs or resistance to change.

- Whose growth mindset and innovative culture do you admire? What are they doing differently? What can you learn from them?

CHAPTER 9

MICHELIN MAGIC

You know what's *never* bittersweet? Dining at a Michelin star restaurant – until you get the bill, that is.

I love food – researching it, photographing it, shopping for it. I'm not too bad at cooking it, but much prefer eating it – especially if it's at a 'one to remember for a lifetime' restaurant.

Dining at a Michelin star restaurant can be a transformative experience. It's not just about the food, although that is certainly a major part of it. It's about the entire experience – the ambiance, the service, the attention to detail. As someone who is passionate about building successful teams and businesses, dining at a Michelin star restaurant has taught me some valuable lessons that I have applied to my work as a change management consultant.

One of the most important lessons is the power of a great team. From the host who greets you at the door to the sommelier who helps you select the perfect wine pairing, every member of the team is critical to creating a flawless dining experience. Each person has their own unique role to play, but they work together seamlessly as a cohesive whole. Watching them in action, it's clear that they share a common goal: to provide the best possible experience for their guests.

Another lesson I've learned is the importance of attention to detail. In a Michelin star restaurant, every element of the dining experience has been carefully thought out, from the placement of the silverware, to the lighting, to the way the plates are presented. No detail is too small to be overlooked. This level of attention to detail is what sets the best restaurants apart from the rest – and it's what sets the best businesses apart, too.

Finally, dining at a Michelin star restaurant has taught me the importance of continuous improvement. Even restaurants that are at the top of their game are constantly seeking ways to improve and innovate. They're never satisfied with the status quo, and they're always looking for ways to push the envelope and exceed their guests' expectations. This is a mindset that is critical for anyone who wants to succeed in business or in life.

Who does this well in the business world? Here are some examples:

- Pixar animation studio is renowned for its attention to detail in creating animated films that appeal to both adults and children. Pixar's success can be attributed to its team-based approach to filmmaking, where every member of the team contributes their unique skills to create a cohesive and engaging final product.

- The Ritz-Carlton luxury hotel chain is known for its exceptional customer service and attention to detail. The company has a strong culture of teamwork and collaboration, with employees trained to anticipate guests' needs and collaborate across departments to provide the best possible experience.

- SpaceX space exploration company has achieved remarkable success in its mission to make space exploration more accessible and affordable. SpaceX's focus on teamwork and attention to detail has enabled the company to develop reusable rockets and achieve significant milestones in their industry.

Dining at a Michelin star restaurant was a humbling and inspiring experience. It reminded me that success is not just about having the right tools or resources, but about building the right team, paying attention to detail and continuously striving for the stars.

Transformative in Tokyo

I remember the feeling of awe that washed over me as I sat down for dinner at that Michelin star restaurant in Tokyo. It wasn't just the stunning view of the city skyline from the 38th floor of the Mandarin

Oriental that took my breath away; It was the whole dining experience that was unforgettable.

As soon as I took my seat I was presented with a tiny toolbox. The contents of this toolbox were miniature versions of hammers, shovels, tweezers and a tape measure, all of which seemed far too small to be of any practical use in a kitchen. However, as the meal progressed, it became clear that these tools were essential for creating the culinary masterpieces that were about to be served.

The first dish arrived, and I watched in amazement as the chef prepared it right in front of me. What seemed like a simple dish on paper was transformed into a work of art through the skilled use of these culinary tools that you'd find in every restaurant kitchen. Every movement was precise, every ingredient was placed with care and every dish was a symphony of flavours and textures.

The dishes became more complex and intricate as the meal progressed. Each one was more impressive than the last, and I couldn't help but marvel at the chefs' creativity and ingenuity. They were able to take raw ingredients and turn them into something truly magical, using nothing more than their skills, regular kitchen tools and a deep understanding of flavour and technique.

When we think of great restaurants, we often think of the Michelin star greats – those that push the boundaries of culinary creativity and bring diners on a journey of flavour and texture. But what makes these restaurants truly exceptional is not just the ingredients' quality or the chefs' skill – it's the structure and organisation behind the scenes that enables the chefs to work their magic.

Just like a Michelin kitchen, organisations need to have clear structures in place to function at their best. Each person needs to know their role, where they fit into the larger picture and what their responsibilities are. This clarity allows for a smooth and efficient operation, with each person contributing their unique skills and expertise.

Just as a Michelin kitchen is segmented by process or dish, organisations can be structured according to geography, function or project. This allows for specialisation and expertise to be developed, leading to greater efficiency and effectiveness.

But successful structures don't just rely on segmentation. Clarity around roles and responsibilities is key to ensuring that everyone is on the same page and working towards the same goals. When people are unsure of their role in a transformation, it can lead to confusion, resistance and, ultimately, failure.

Just like the chefs in a Michelin kitchen use tools to create culinary masterpieces, organisations need to have the right tools and resources to achieve their goals. This could be anything from software systems to training programs to financial resources. But just like the tiny toolbox presented to me at that Tokyo restaurant, it's not about the size or complexity of the tools – it's about how they are used.

Finally, a Michelin kitchen relies on the chefs' skill and expertise – and organisations need to have the right people in place with the right skills and expertise to achieve their goals. This means not only hiring the right people, but also investing in their development and creating the conditions that allow them to thrive.

The same elements that make a great restaurant – raw ingredients, the right tools and resources, skilled and motivated people – can be applied to any organisation. But it's not enough to simply have these elements in place; they need to be combined in a way that creates something greater than the sum of its parts.

The magic of Michelin

Michelin star restaurant chefs truly are like magicians. They possess the unique ability to seamlessly blend the left and right brain – the analytical and the creative – to produce culinary masterpieces that not only taste amazing but also look visually stunning. The process of creating a dish in a Michelin star restaurant involves both imagination and technical expertise. The chefs use their creativity, storytelling skills and theatrics to transform a raw ingredient into a work of art, while at the same time relying on food science, supply chain smarts and ingredient utilisation to ensure that the dish is not only visually appealing, but tastes amazing and is profitable.

This is not so different from building a successful organisation. Just like Michelin star restaurants, organisations have access to the same inputs including people, process and technology (see table 9.1). In a restaurant, there is the executive chef who leads the kitchen team, the maître d' who manages the front of house and the sommelier who curates the wine list. In an organisation, there is the CEO who leads the company, direct reports who manage different departments and a variety of specialists in areas such as marketing, finance, IT and procurement.

> **WHEN DIGITAL TRANSFORMATION IS DONE RIGHT, IT'S LIKE A CATERPILLAR TURNING INTO A BUTTERFLY, BUT WHEN DONE WRONG, ALL YOU HAVE IS A REALLY FAST CATERPILLAR.**
>
> GEORGE WESTERMAN

Table 9.1: Restaurants versus organisations

	Restaurant	Organisation
People	Executive chef Sous chef Maître d' Sommelier Host Food scientist	CEO and their direct reports Marketing Finance IT Communications Procurement
Process	Frying Grilling Flambéing Baking Poaching Fileting	Applying for leave Completing a performance appraisal Starting a new joiner induction Conducting an exit interview Annual business planning

Tech	Electric knife
	Thermomix
	Sous-vide
	Freeze drier
	Blow torch
		Enterprise resource planning (ERP) software
		Customer relationship management (CRM)
		   software
		Human resources information system
		   (HRIS)
		Microsoft Office suite

Both restaurants and organisations need to have the right people in the right roles, with the necessary skills and expertise to achieve their goals. In a restaurant, the chef and their team need to have the culinary expertise to cook a delicious meal. In an organisation, employees need to have the right skills to perform their jobs efficiently and effectively.

THE PRICE OF DOING THE SAME OLD THING IS FAR HIGHER THAN THE PRICE OF CHANGE.

BILL CLINTON

Processes are crucial in both restaurants and organisations. In a restaurant, the chef needs to have a clear and efficient process for cooking each dish. In an organisation, employees need to follow well-defined processes to complete tasks such as applying for leave, conducting an exit interview or completing a performance appraisal.

Technology is also a critical ingredient in both restaurants and organisations. In a restaurant, technology such as sous-vide machines and freeze dryers help the chef to create new and innovative dishes. In an organisation, tech platforms can help to streamline processes and increase productivity.

To create magic in any organisation, you need to start with the raw ingredients – the people, the tools and the resources. These are all essential ingredients, but it's the way they are combined and used that determines the final outcome. An organisation can create something truly magical.

No pressure, no diamonds

What I've come to realise is that Michelin star kitchens are culinary autoclaves.

They ingest inputs and add more passion, pressure and precision beyond what is 'normal' to produce an abnormally stellar result.

The pressure comes from the exceptional standards they aim to uphold, not because it's a manic overbearing soul-destroying environment. There's an eerie calm in many Michelin kitchens where each person is solely focused on their part in bringing a dish to fruition.

This is what separates reality stars from the legit Michelin stars.

Michelin restaurants have an uncompromising commitment to exceptional standards and quite a unique perspective on failure. Failure is not defined as creating a poorly executed dish; it's defined by *passing on* a poorly executed dish to a patron.

A Michelin nightmare is a poorly executed dish getting through the goalie, followed by the mortification of having to recall said dish. A Michelin dream is upholding Michelin standards even if a dish must be redone a number of times.

Each person on the line knows their role, knows what they contribute and knows what 'good' looks like so they can ensure that's executed before the dish is passed on to the next artist. This encourages a culture of attention to detail and accountability, where every team member takes ownership of their part in the process and works to ensure the final product meets the high standards. The shared passion for excellence and pride in their work is so strong that they opt into all the trappings and demands characteristic of a Michelin standard.

The concept of adding pressure to produce exceptional results is not limited to Michelin star kitchens. In fact, many successful companies have adopted a similar philosophy. By setting and upholding high standards, these organisations push their employees to go above and beyond what is expected, resulting in outstanding performance and unparalleled innovation.

WHEN PRESSURE IS APPLIED IN A CONSTRUCTIVE WAY, WITH CLEAR GOALS AND SUPPORT FROM MANAGEMENT, IT CAN LEAD TO INCREDIBLE SUCCESS.

However, it is important to note the fine line between healthy pressure and an insanely stressful environment. When pressure is applied in a constructive way, with clear goals and support from management, it can lead to incredible success. But when it becomes overwhelming and stressful, it can have the opposite effect and lead to burnout and turnover.

THE FUTURE FIT ORGANISATION

To create a culture of healthy pressure, organisations should clearly communicate expectations, providing the necessary resources and support for employees to meet those expectations and recognising and rewarding exceptional performance. This creates a sense of shared purpose and pride in the work, leading to a more engaged and motivated workforce.

When it comes to creating enterprise-wide change, we must redefine failure in a way that encourages continuous improvement and learning. The most effective organisations reframe failure as feedback. Here are some examples of those who do it well:

- Toyota has a well-known approach to quality and continuous improvement called the Toyota Production System. This approach focuses on eliminating waste, improving efficiency and empowering employees to take ownership of their work.

- Zappos online shoe and clothing retailer is known for its customer service and company culture. Zappos has a WOW philosophy, where employees are encouraged to go above and beyond to create a positive customer experience.

- Singapore Airlines has consistently been ranked as one of the world's best airlines, in part due to its attention to detail and commitment to customer service. The airline's Singapore Girl branding that embodies grace, elegance, and attention to detail.

Adding pressure can indeed produce 'diamonds' in an organisation, but it must be done in a healthy and constructive way, with clear goals, support and a supportive culture that encourages failing fast.

> **WE WENT FROM BEING THE FLINTSTONES TO THE JETSONS IN NINE MONTHS.**
>
> DAN SCHULMAN

PAUSE AND REFLECT

- How does the dynamic of a high-performing team in a Michelin star restaurant mirror a healthy and successful organisation? Reflect on the importance of clear roles and responsibilities, effective communication, collaboration, trust and a shared commitment to excellence in achieving outstanding results.

- What can you learn from the teamwork and collaboration observed in Michelin star restaurants to enhance your own team's performance? Reflect on the practices of fostering a culture of accountability, continuous improvement, and mutual support, as well as creating an environment where diverse perspectives are valued, and individuals are encouraged to contribute their unique skills and expertise.

- What would skyrocket your team's cohesion? What safeguards or structures need to be in place to unlock their hidden potential? Reflect on strategies to promote cross-functional collaboration, empower teams to take ownership of change initiatives, foster a climate of psychological safety that encourages innovation and risk-taking, and recognise and reward collective achievements.

CHAPTER 10

CULINARY CODE CRACKERS

The Michelin world has cracked the code. The restaurants bestowed those coveted stars set the gold standard for culinary excellence, and their approach to building a successful team is worth emulating in any industry. The key takeaway is that the right people are the foundation of any great organisation.

Michelin restaurants know this all too well. Why?

Michelin stars are awarded to a restaurant *as a whole*. It's about the complete experience, and no-one knows when a Michelin inspector will visit. A 'starred' chef transferring to another restaurant won't take 'their' star with them. A highly competent maître d' or chef sommelier who quits may very well cost a restaurant a star, and hiring world-class people could be the last detail that finally pushes a restaurant over the threshold to earn one.

In the Michelin world, everyone is important. Everyone has a part to play. The recruitment process starts with a clear vision of what the restaurant is trying to achieve. This is followed by an exhaustive search for people who share that vision and embody it in their work ethic, attitude and talent. The emphasis is not just on finding the most experienced or talented chefs, but on building a team of people who are unified by a shared philosophy of excellence.

Once the right team is assembled, the restaurant sets about fortifying their people with everything they need to succeed. This includes providing the best possible support, systems and structures to help them excel. Those in the Michelin world understand that success is not just about having the right tools, but also about having the right team that can use those tools to their full potential.

The same is true for digital transformation in any organisation. Success is not just about having the latest technology or the best digital tools. It's about having the right people who can leverage those tools to create real value. This means finding the right combination of skills and experience and creating a shared philosophy of excellence that everyone can embrace.

To achieve this, organisations need to take a people-first approach to digital transformation. This means investing in the right people with the right skills and giving them the support, structure and systems they need to succeed. As illustrated by figure 10.1, the four quadrants of sustainable change must be present for an organisation to sustain transformational change efforts.

If you only have support and skills, change is not sustained or turned into 'business as usual'. If you only have support and systems, you'll have frustrated leaders and employees won't feel ready or able to change. If you only have systems and structures there will be a lack of adoption and buy-in. If you only have systems and skills you'll wind up with frustrated employees, and leaders who don't buy in.

Figure 10.1: The four quadrants of sustainable change

Support Leadership equipped to role model and advocate for change	Skills People given opportunity to level-up skill sets that enable change
Systems The change process is systemised to enable change to occur at scale with less effort	Structures Change is integrated into the business through workflows, job descriptions, remuneration policies and so on

Systems and structures are critical to achieving consistency. By being consistent, you reduce errors and unexpected surprises and minimise cost blowouts. Earning a Michelin star is hard. And maintaining it year after year? Even harder! 'Consistency between visits' is a rumoured selection criteria, which means having the right structures and people in place is non-negotiable.

SYSTEMS AND STRUCTURES ARE CRITICAL TO ACHIEVING CONSISTENCY.

By following the Michelin world's example and focusing on the people stack, organisations can create a team that is truly capable of magic. They can create a culture of excellence that inspires everyone to reach new heights, and they can drive real value from their digital transformation efforts. The key is to remember that success is not just about the tools you have, but also about the people who use them.

There are many examples of companies that have done this well. Mindvalley, a Malaysia-based personal development company, offers online courses and programs in wellness, productivity and leadership. It places a strong emphasis on employee development and offers regular training sessions and personal coaching to improve how its people use its own suite of personal development tools.

> **WE TALK ABOUT AUTOMATING OPERATIONS, ABOUT PEOPLE, AND ABOUT NEW BUSINESS MODELS. WRAPPED INSIDE THOSE TOPICS ARE DATA ANALYTICS, TECHNOLOGIES, AND SOFTWARE – ALL OF WHICH ARE ENABLERS, NOT DRIVERS. IN THE CENTER OF IT ALL IS LEADERSHIP AND CULTURE. UNDERSTANDING WHAT DIGITAL MEANS TO YOUR COMPANY – WHETHER YOU'RE A FINANCIAL, AGRICULTURAL, PHARMACEUTICAL, OR RETAIL INSTITUTION – IS ESSENTIAL.**
>
> JIM SWANSON

Canada-based travel company G Adventures is known for its small-group adventure tours around the world. It offers leadership training, language classes and global exchange programs to its staff to ensure they know the company's own offerings intimately and can speak to customers with conviction.

Social media management company Buffer is known for its remote work culture and commitment to transparency and employee wellbeing. It offers regular feedback and coaching, access to outside education and training and an annual personal development stipend for each employee.

Top-down support

Any change needs to be supported at the very top – to ensure it lasts. If the CEO and senior leadership team aren't on board with any changes relating to building your future fitness, save yourself the trouble and go back to bed.

To ensure that the desired change is adopted and sustained throughout the organisation, leaders must not only support it but also model the behaviours they wish to see in their employees. This can involve providing training opportunities, offering personal development initiatives and coaching employees to enact the necessary behaviour change.

The Michelin star restaurant is a rare breed in a world full of mediocrity and 'good enough' establishments. In chapter 9 I introduced what sets a Michelin star restaurant apart from other restaurants: when a dish is deemed not to meet the agreed standard for excellence it is not able to be served. It is simply tossed out. There's no blaming, no finger pointing and no judgement; they just quickly start over and get it right the second time.

This rarely happens in organisations. Especially in large companies, a post-mortem or retrospective occurs where the causes of what went wrong are examined in great detail. This has a time and place, of course – it's important to reflect on lessons learned and what could be done better next time (or how to avoid the issue occurring in the first place).

What does *not* have a time and place today, or in the future, is a lack of accountability. This is where the blame game and shifting of the onus of responsibility runs rampant.

WHAT DOES NOT HAVE A TIME AND PLACE TODAY IS A LACK OF ACCOUNTABILITY.

The executive chef's commitment to excellence means that any dish that does not meet their standards is quickly discarded and redone, without blame. This level of accountability is rarely seen in organisations, where there's a tendency to assign blame for what went wrong. Instead, Michelin star leaders take responsibility and support their employees to make the necessary changes to improve performance.

Ultimately, the key to successful transformation is having leaders who not only support but actively champion the desired changes. Leaders must be willing to model the behaviours they expect from their employees and provide the necessary support to make those changes stick. With top-down support, the entire organisation can work towards building future fitness and achieving sustained success.

One example of a failed transformation due to lack of leadership support is former video rental giant Blockbuster. In the early 2000s, Blockbuster had the opportunity to acquire Netflix for only $50 million, but the CEO at the time, John Antioco, refused the offer. He didn't see the potential in the emerging online streaming market and instead chose to stick with Blockbuster's bricks-and-mortar rental model.

We know how the story ends. Blockbuster fell behind its competitors and was unable to adapt to the changing market. The company filed for bankruptcy in 2010, and today only one Blockbuster store remains in operation. In this case, a lack of leadership support for innovation and new technologies led to the downfall of a once-successful company.

Changing an organisation's culture is not for the faint-hearted. Culture change initiatives have an extremely high failure rate because they rely on 100 per cent senior leadership alignment, sponsorship, commitment and accountability. Successful change means making tough decisions such as letting go of toxic 'high performers', enforcing a strict 'no dickheads' policy no matter how desperate you may be for a certain skill set, and enforcing consequences for managers who refuse to get on the bus. It's a rare leader who has the persistence, integrity and alignment between what they say and what they do.

> **I ALONE CANNOT CHANGE THE WORLD, BUT I CAN CAST A STONE ACROSS THE WATERS TO CREATE MANY RIPPLES.**
>
> **MOTHER TERESA**

Leaders need to live it, believe it, become it. They need to role model the change they want to see permeate through the organisation. Leaders need to support change. They also need to provide support to others in the organisation to adopt the change.

Let's look at what true support from a leader looks like.

Communicate the vision and benefits
A leader needs to communicate the reasons behind the change, what is changing, what the benefits are to the organisation and how individuals may be impacted. This helps employees understand the rationale so they are more likely to get on board. The *why* is the most important message to disseminate.

Ever had a delayed flight? An hour passes, two hours pass, and you still don't know why? It's frustrating beyond belief. Same with organisational change. Help your people understand why the change is happening and when, and you'll relieve a lot of their stress.

A common mistake I've witnessed, particularly in large transformations, is leaders delegating responsibilities they should take care of themselves – such as communicating directly with employees, managing toxic people and developing support for change through formal and informal relationships.

Lead by example
A leader needs to set an example by embracing the change themselves. This demonstrates that the change is important and worth adopting.

While working for a large utilities company I was responsible for implementing a change in vehicle car pooling. The change was driven by the need to consolidate vehicles and improve compliance by tracking fuel mileage and travel (it was widely known that some employees were abusing their privilege, using company cars to run personal errands such as grocery shopping and picking up the kids from school).

It was not a popular change. In fact, it was so contentious rumours were flying that the unions would get involved to disrupt business through organised strikes. Luckily, the CEO was a people person, liked and respected by many. He made a huge impact on the success of this change by being the first to hand in his vehicle. He gave an impassioned speech about pulling together and doing what's best for the company, which would ultimately benefit the community overall. He made the front page of the newspaper, and many other high-profile leaders followed suit.

Provide support and resources

A leader needs to ensure that employees have the resources they need to adapt to the change. This includes training, technology and additional support as needed.

Change doesn't happen with a click of the fingers. Make sure you have a change management expert who is well versed in creating artefacts and deliverables that shorten the skill gap.

RESOURCES ALSO MEAN THE PROVISION OF TIME. PEOPLE NEED TO GET USED TO THE CHANGE, AND HAVE SPACE TO PRACTISE NEW SKILLS IN A 'SAFE TO FAIL' ENVIRONMENT.

Resources also mean the provision of time. People need to get used to the change, and have space to practise new skills in a 'safe to fail' environment.

Think of an aeroplane pilot. The hours a pilot needs to train in a flight simulator before flying a real plane varies depending on the type of aircraft and the specific requirements of the airline or aviation authority. For example, according to the US Federal Aviation Administration, pilots need to complete a minimum of 25 hours of simulator training before flying an Airbus A320, and a minimum of 35 hours of simulator training before flying a Boeing 737. Similarly, the European Aviation Safety Agency requires pilots to complete a minimum of 32 hours of simulator training before flying an Airbus A320, and a minimum of 40 hours of simulator training before flying a Boeing 737.

When I was leading a 'heart and lung' technology implementation for an emergency services client, I organised for a 'sandpit environment' to be created. The system being replaced was one that tracked, managed and audited all triple-zero calls for police and emergency assistance. Imagine incorrectly sending a police helicopter in the wrong direction, or dispatching a fleet of cars to the wrong house. The stakes were literally life and death, and having a replica tool where call takers could practise responding to triple-zero calls enabled them to confidently build their proficiency without risking unintentional harm to the community.

Empower and involve employees

A leader should involve employees in the change process, seeking their input and ideas. This empowers employees to take ownership of the change and contribute to its success.

Here's how Whole Foods Market did it. Whole Foods is known for its decentralised management structure. Employees have a lot of autonomy and decision-making power at the store level. This means that when changes are being implemented, employees are often involved in the process from the beginning.

For example, in 2015, Whole Foods announced that it would be rolling out a new store-level inventory management system. Rather than simply imposing the new system on employees, the company worked with them to design and test it. A cross-departmental project team was formed, spending months testing the system and providing feedback to the developers.

This collaborative approach paid off: after the new system was implemented, the company saw a 10 per cent improvement in inventory accuracy, which helped reduce waste and improve profitability.

I've experienced the power of employee involvement personally. One of my clients, a large international engineering consultancy, had tried many times in the past to gain traction for a new five-year strategy – unsuccessfully. The new strategy was always met with unenthusiastic head nods and tight smiles. There were no straight-out refusals, but there also wasn't any enthusiasm or behaviour change.

The client agreed with my recommendation to go deeper into the organisation to solicit opinions and views. A structured interview was developed, and a combination of one-on-one interviews with senior leaders and cross-organisation focus groups were scheduled for the following two months. The results were analysed, calibrated and reflected back to the business.

In many of the focus groups, people got emotional. They said they had never been asked for their views before, especially not on a topic as important as their new five-year strategy. After these focus groups, I facilitated a session for the top 100 leaders to gain alignment and endorsement of the newly revised strategy, each and every table stated 'positive' as the key emotion they felt when they thought about the future of the organisation. It was unanimous, and they all committed to individual actions to drive the strategy forward. This was the first time that had happened in the company's history.

Involving employees in the change process can help build buy-in and engagement, improve the quality of the final product and strengthen relationships bi-directionally.

Celebrate successes

A leader should acknowledge and celebrate successes along the way, no matter how small. This helps build momentum and reinforces the positive impact of the change.

When employees feel valued and recognised, they are more likely to continue to invest their time and energy into making the change effort a success. Celebrating successes helps build a more positive cohesive culture within the organisation.

HubSpot does this well. It regularly celebrates small wins and successes, both through formal recognition programs and informal celebrations. For example, the company has a Kudos program, where employees give each other public recognition for their contributions. The company also regularly celebrates milestones such as hitting revenue targets or launching new products.

This focus on celebrating successes has helped to build a positive and motivated culture at HubSpot, leading to high levels of engagement and retention. It has also helped to maintain momentum for change within the organisation, as employees are continually motivated to make improvements and achieve new goals.

Celebrating wins is positively correlated with an organisation's ability to maintain momentum and motivation for change. Leaders should recognise and value the contributions of all employees to inspire continued effort, especially in the case of multiyear transformations.

A leader should be a champion for the change, demonstrating their commitment and dedication to making it successful, and supporting their team throughout the process.

Structuring for success

A Michelin star kitchen is a well-oiled machine.

Each person knows their role, where they exist in the chain, how a dish should look when it arrives at their station and how it should look when it leaves. Just as organisations can be structured according to geography and function, so too can Michelin star restaurants be segmented by process (such as grilling, frying or flambéing) or by course.

A strong structure requires a high level of clarity around everyone's roles and responsibilities. Where change falls flat, it's often because people were unaware of, or not owning, their role in the transformation.

NOT EVERYTHING THAT IS FACED CAN BE CHANGED, BUT NOTHING CAN BE CHANGED UNTIL IT IS FACED.

JAMES BALDWIN

Structural realignment
Leaders must ensure that their structures are aligned with the transformation goals and objectives, and that everyone in the organisation is aware of how they can

contribute to its success. They should align and integrate individual key performance indicators and goals with the change. This approach can be applied to any kind of change, whether it's implementing new technology or restructuring teams.

When I was involved in a US$450-million-plus global offshoring program for a top tier engineering company, I had to change how project managers were incentivised and remunerated.

The change was significant: a new company mandate to send any non-critical non-client-facing work traditionally done by engineers and draughtspeople in the US, UK, Canada and Australia to lower-cost countries such as China and India. It would save the organisation 30 per cent in costs annually.

Adoption was non-existent. Why? The program failed to assess the people in charge of resourcing the work – the project managers. What's in it for them? What's important to them? What are the forces for and against this change?

When I undertook some analysis, I discovered the project managers' bonuses were linked to client satisfaction – not total project cost or percentage of offshore resources used. It's no wonder the project managers weren't on board!

I partnered with HR to ensure the project managers' benefits were changed to align with the transformation. It was a chunky piece of work that took an additional few months to complete, but set the project up for success. Adoption crept up, and by the midyear check-point most regions were achieving their targets.

British Airways is another example of a company that changed its underpinning structures to align with its transformation program. In the late 1990s, British Airways was facing tough competition from low-cost carriers, and was struggling with high costs and low profitability. To turn the company around, then CEO Bob Ayling initiated major changes such as streamlining the company's fleet and reducing staff numbers.

As part of this effort, Ayling also implemented a new reporting structure that decentralised decision-making, empowering more and more frontline employees. This newly aligned structure allowed employees to have more ownership over their work and fostered a more innovative and entrepreneurial culture.

British Airways also introduced a new performance management system that tied employee bonuses to customer satisfaction scores, which further incentivised employees to prioritise customer experience. These changes transformed British Airways into a more customer-focused and financially successful airline. By the early 2000s, British Airways had returned to profitability and was recognised for its strong customer service and innovative business practices.

SUCCESSFUL TRANSFORMATIONS REQUIRE A CLEAR AND WELL-STRUCTURED APPROACH, WITH EVERYONE IN THE ORGANISATION AWARE OF THEIR ROLE AND RESPONSIBILITIES.

Successful transformations require everyone in the organisation being aware of their role and responsibilities. Leaders must ensure that their structures are aligned with the transformational goals and objectives, and that everyone is aware of the benefits of the change. By taking a structured approach to transformation, organisations can ensure that they are future fit and well positioned to compete in an increasingly dynamic and challenging business environment.

All systems go

Systems play a critical role in driving performance and results in organisations. A system is a set of interconnected processes that work together to achieve a specific goal. In a Michelin star kitchen, the systemisation of operations ensures consistency. This allows the restaurant to maintain a high level of excellence in service, quality and experience. It also helps save costs, reduces waste and prevents unexpected surprises and glitches.

The importance of systems is not just limited to the culinary world. It applies to all industries, and is essential in digital transformation. Systemising digital transformation helps to ensure that new and emerging technologies are rolled out efficiently and effectively. It involves defining a set of processes and procedures that enable you to identify and respond to changes quickly and effectively.

Here's an example of systems in practice. Maersk, a Danish shipping and logistics company, implemented a comprehensive digital transformation program to increase efficiency and productivity across its operations. As part of this program, the company implemented a system to track and monitor performance metrics for each of the digital transformation initiatives. This system provided real-time data on the progress of each initiative, allowing the company to quickly identify and address any issues that arose during the implementation process. It also allowed the company to measure the impact of the initiatives on key performance indicators, such as cost savings, customer satisfaction, and employee engagement.

By systemising the change management process in this way, Maersk was able to achieve significant improvements in its operations, including a 20 per cent reduction in supply chain costs and a 15 per cent increase in customer satisfaction. The company also saw increased employee engagement and innovation, as employees were empowered to identify and implement process improvements using the data the system provided.

In chapter 6 I told you about my experience leading the change effort at a large gold miner. This required systemising many elements of change management. Adoption and engagement data was systematically collected and analysed to make step-change improvements in how future technologies were rolled out. The systemised data collation covered aspects such as login and use time on certain applications, completion of training and tasks, and qualitative data obtained through observation, peer feedback and surveys. This data was used to determine which step of the process or tool users found problematic or most useful, who the star performers were and who the loafers were. With this information, leaders could acknowledge and recognise high achievers, which would boost motivation to change even more.

A 30-SECOND ENCOUNTER WITH A LEADER CAN MAKE A SIGNIFICANT IMPACT ON EMPLOYEE MOTIVATION.

A 30-second encounter with a leader can make a significant impact on employee motivation. Recognition from a leader, whether in person or remote, can ignite motivation to change like wildfire. This is why it's so important for leaders to create systems that enable them to recognise and acknowledge employees who are making a difference in the organisation regularly. It's not about providing bonuses or a ping-pong table, but giving recognition that helps employees feel valued and appreciated – and gets them adopting change.

Regardless of the industry you're working in, systems are critical in driving performance and results. Leaders must recognise the importance of creating systems that enable them to identify and respond to changes quickly, to ensure that new and emerging technologies are rolled out efficiently and effectively. Finally, leaders must systemise how they acknowledge and recognise employees who are the early adopters of change in the organisation to whet the appetite for more change.

PAUSE AND REFLECT

- How well developed are your skills and capabilities in change leadership, sponsorship and communication? How can you further develop them?

- How effectively are the existing structures and systems in your organisation supporting the desired transformation? Reflect on the alignment of roles, responsibilities and processes with the transformation goals, and consider any necessary adjustments or improvements to create an enabling environment.

- What support mechanisms are in place to facilitate and sustain the transformation efforts? Reflect on the availability of resources, training, mentorship and coaching to support individuals and teams throughout the transformation journey. Consider how to foster a culture of continuous learning, feedback and collaboration to ensure ongoing support for growth and development.

CHAPTER 11

THE PRISM PRINCIPLE

I've built a career around change, enabling large-scale behaviour change in some of the biggest names in mining, engineering and technology. What I've learned is that building an organisation's future fitness needs more than a long list of credentials and certifications. To truly excel in today's rapidly changing business environment, it's essential to embrace three key principles: prism, play and production.

A prism is a glass object, triangular with refracting surfaces at an acute angle from each other and separates white light into a spectrum of colours. The term 'prism' is also used to refer to the clarification or distortion afforded by a particular viewpoint.

In an organisational context, 'prism' refers to the ability to see things from multiple perspectives and to recognise the interconnectedness of different systems and stakeholders. It involves understanding the complexities and nuances of the business environment and using this knowledge to make informed decisions and take strategic action.

If we view tech-enabled transformation through the prism of human experience, it refracts into a rainbow of possibilities.

It's all about how you see it

Conventional thinking leads to recurring problems. If you have a lack of focus on people and a narrow lens on technical measures in digital transformation, you will fail to consider the needs and skills of the various stakeholders who are critical to your success.

Conventional thinking tends to prioritise 'hard' measures such as hours, speed and feeds in assessing the digital transformation success, but this focus on technology alone can come at the expense of people. The people element is often the last thought – or, worse, is forgotten altogether.

Instead of asking 'how much?' when assessing a digital transformation program, executives should ask how a digital transformation program can help them go from where they are to their desired destination, and the people needed to achieve it.

Even if (by some miracle) the people stack is considered early, many organisations make the mistake of including or considering the needs and skills of only one type of person, such as technical staff.

A people-focused (as opposed to problem-focused) approach to digital transformation is paramount. It recognises that technology alone cannot bring about successful digital transformation. It prioritises the needs of the people who are at the centre of the change (whether that's employees or customers) and cultivates a culture of engagement, collaboration and innovation that change can be driven

> **EVERY INDUSTRY AND EVERY ORGANISATION WILL HAVE TO TRANSFORM ITSELF IN THE NEXT FEW YEARS. WHAT IS COMING AT US IS BIGGER THAN THE ORIGINAL INTERNET AND YOU NEED TO UNDERSTAND IT, GET ON BOARD WITH IT AND FIGURE OUT HOW TO TRANSFORM YOUR BUSINESS.**
>
> TIM O'REILLY

from within. Here are some examples of companies that have adopted this people-focused approach:

- **Increased buy-in:** When employees are involved in the digital transformation process from the beginning, they are more likely to be invested in its success. Bupa, a UK-based healthcare provider, involved employees at all levels in its digital transformation journey. The company established an internal innovation lab that invited all employees to participate in, identifying new opportunities to innovate.

- **Improved collaboration:** A people-focused approach to digital transformation promotes collaboration and communication between teams, departments and individuals. This can help to break down silos and create a culture of innovation and cross-functional cooperation. German multinational conglomerate Siemens embraced a people-focused approach when it introduced a new digital platform across its global operations. The company created a cross-functional team of employees from different departments to collaborate on its design and implementation. This ensured the platform catered and met the needs of all employees.

- **Greater innovation:** A people-focused approach can foster a culture of innovation that encourages employees to explore new ways of working and identify opportunities for growth. German multinational engineering and technology company Bosch launched a company-wide innovation initiative, inviting all employees to submit their ideas for new digital products and services. The initiative led to the development of new ideas that helped to drive the company's digital transformation.

> **SLOWNESS TO CHANGE USUALLY MEANS FEAR OF THE NEW.**
>
> PHIL CROSBY

A people-focused approach to digital transformation is essential for success. This involves considering the needs and skills of all stakeholders and ensuring that a diverse range of perspectives are included in the decision-making process. By doing so, the likelihood of successfully navigating the challenges of digital transformation by having a workforce that actually wants to drive change from within is significantly higher.

Diversity done right

Diversity is not just the right thing to do, it's the thing we have to do right. It's a crucial factor in the success of digital transformation initiatives. By embracing a diverse range of skills, experiences, and perspectives, organisations can ensure they have a large toolkit to tackle the complex challenges of tomorrow.

> **DIVERSITY IS NOT JUST THE RIGHT THING TO DO, IT'S THE THING WE HAVE TO DO RIGHT.**

A diverse team brings a range of skills and experiences that can foster unique and innovative solutions to complex problems. Diverse teams are also more likely to reflect the diverse needs of the customer base, leading to better customer understanding and engagement. Having a diverse team can also help to break down groupthink, encouraging critical thinking and better decision-making.

When Microsoft set out to improve its product accessibility, it formed a diverse team that included people with disabilities, accessibility advocates and product engineers. The team members used their diverse perspectives to identify and prioritise issues that needed to be addressed, resulting in more inclusive products for all users.

When people from different cultural backgrounds work together, they bring with them unique perspectives and approaches that generate more innovative solutions than would otherwise be discovered. This is particularly important in digital transformation initiatives that require never-before-trialled ideas.

Diversity also encompasses the full spectrum of cognitive ability and human emotion. A successful digital transformation initiative needs more than just coders and programmers. It requires people who can communicate effectively, collaborate, think creatively and influence others to adapt to change. By embracing diversity, organisations can bring together people with complementary skills and strengths to create a holistic strategy of encouraging widespread adoption and integration of new and emerging technologies.

In my experience, as the rate of organisational change and technology increases, so too does the need for effective interpersonal communication skills. Pumble reports that neglecting employees' needs to be heard and recognised can lead to poor performance results.[36] It quotes Grammarly's, *The State of Business Communications 2023* report, which cites ineffective communication as a barrier to inclusion, with 69 per cent of surveyed workers reporting feeling stressed due to unclear communication.[37]

Organisations must ensure a significant part of their workforce has the skills to communicate effectively across cultures and departments.

The F word

Why are feelings rarely talked about in the workplace?

Bringing feelings into the workplace is important. It enables people to connect on a deeper level and understand each other better. When emotions are ignored or dismissed, this leads to a lack of trust, communication breakdowns and low morale. It's important to recognise that emotions are a natural and normal part of the human experience, and they should be acknowledged and expressed in a healthy and constructive way.

Emotions are often labelled as positive or negative, but this is misleading. All emotions have a purpose, and even so-called negative emotions such as anger and frustration can be used constructively to drive growth and improvement. By acknowledging and accepting all emotions, we can create a more open and honest workplace where people feel comfortable expressing themselves.

Building emotional intelligence (EQ) is crucial for effective digital transformation. EQ helps us understand and manage our own and others' emotions. This is particularly important during times of change, when resistance is a common response. By recognising and managing resistance, we can minimise its impact and move forward with the transformation more quickly.

Novo Nordisk has leveraged its organisational EQ to drive progress. The Danish pharmaceutical company has a strong culture of empathy and emotional intelligence. The company's purpose is to drive change to defeat diabetes and other serious chronic diseases such as obesity and rare blood and endocrine disorders. To achieve this goal, Novo Nordisk places a high value on understanding the needs and experiences of patients and healthcare providers. Employees are encouraged to build relationships based on empathy and respect, to work collaboratively to find innovative solutions to healthcare challenges and to dedicate time to experiment with cutting-edge technologies.

> **WE NEED TO GIVE EACH OTHER THE SPACE TO GROW, TO BE OURSELVES, TO EXERCISE OUR DIVERSITY. WE NEED TO GIVE EACH OTHER SPACE SO THAT WE MAY BOTH GIVE AND RECEIVE SUCH BEAUTIFUL THINGS AS IDEAS, OPENNESS, DIGNITY, JOY, HEALING, AND INCLUSION.**
>
> **MAX DE PREE**

Incorporating emotional and personality diversity into your people stack is important. It can lead to more creative problem-solving, better decision-making and a more inclusive culture.

Bringing feelings into the workplace and building emotional intelligence are crucial for digital transformation success. By recognising and embracing the full range of human emotions and experiences we increase our relational intelligence, which creates a more understanding and harmonious workplace where differences are embraced.

Diversity is what makes a people stack not only more beautiful, but more likely to succeed.

PAUSE AND REFLECT

- How do you prioritise the human experience when considering technology transformation initiatives? Reflect on the extent to which you involve end users and stakeholders in the design and implementation process so that technology solutions meet their needs and enhance their experience.

- In what ways can you promote empathy and user-centricity during technology transformation? Reflect on the strategies you could employ to gather user feedback and create channels for open communication so that you understand the impact of technology changes on employees, customers and other stakeholders.

- How can you ensure that technology transformation initiatives align with the organisation's values, culture and purpose, while enhancing the overall human experience? Reflect on the ethical considerations, potential impact on job roles and the need for upskilling or reskilling to ensure that technology integration is not only efficient but also aligns with your organisation's human-centric values.

CHAPTER 12

THE PLAY PRINCIPLE

Play is all about fostering creativity and innovation within your organisation. It means having fun while experimenting, risk-taking, learning and growing. When people feel free to play and explore new ideas, they are more likely to come up with innovative solutions to complex challenges.

When you play, especially as a child, you spend time doing an enjoyable or entertaining activity. There's something magical about watching children play. Whether it's with Lego or the latest VR action game, playing dress-ups or pretending they're a storybook character, their curiosity and enthusiasm for exploring the unknown is palpable.

> **UNFORTUNATELY, AS ADULTS, WE'VE FORGOTTEN HOW TO PLAY. WE'VE TRADED OUR CURIOSITY FOR CONTEMPT.**

Unfortunately, as adults, we've forgotten how to play. We've traded our curiosity for contempt. Many workplaces today are very rigid and hierarchical, discouraging employees from taking risks or trying new things. However, there are some companies that have recognised the importance of play and curiosity in driving innovation and success.

One example is Google, which has incorporated play into its company culture. Google's offices are designed to be fun and creative spaces, with amenities such as game rooms, slides, bowling alleys and even dance studios.

Another example is the design firm IDEO, which uses play and experimentation as a key part of its innovation process. IDEO's designers are encouraged to build prototypes of their ideas quickly and test them out. This approach has helped IDEO create some of the most innovative products, such as the first Apple mouse and the shopping cart redesign for Target.

> **THE NEXT FIVE YEARS WILL BE MORE DISRUPTIVE THAN THE LAST 15. THIS IS NOT BUSINESS AS USUAL. A LOT OF TECHNOLOGY THAT CAME IN THREE YEARS AGO DOESN'T WORK ANYMORE.**
>
> **SAUL BERMAN**

These examples suggest that incorporating play and curiosity into work environments can lead to more innovative and successful outcomes. Companies can tap into the creativity and diversity of their employees to drive digital transformation and other types of change.

When curiosity saves the day

One of the most challenging change programs I ever led nearly broke me. It only involved 1000 people, but it may as well have been 1 million. It was for a state fire and emergency services department and involved a new CEO, a bushfire season, a new building, new processes, new branding and new tech.

The new architect-designed smart building was five years late and AU$15 million over budget. It was a beautiful building but it was located far from the city. It was less convenient with fewer amenities and cafes, and fewer public transport options. The tech being introduced was so much more advanced than employees were used to – it was like going from a brick phone to the latest generation iPhone.

Needless to say, resistance was sky high. The predominantly older employee group felt out of their depth. They were scared. They didn't say it, but it's human nature to fear losing something when you're told about a change: losing face, losing reputation, losing money, losing time, losing seniority, losing respect . . . the list goes on.

It was getting toxic. Rumours were swirling and the naysayers seemed to triple in number within weeks.

I had to nip it in the bud. What did I do?

I orchestrated an entire experience. I elicited that childlike curiosity and wonder.

I went to the site of the new building. I literally walked around the surrounding businesses introducing myself, seeing what I could gather that would make my client's employees feel special.

It was quite a haul: free calendars, pens, coffee vouchers, dry cleaner vouchers, special deals and so on. I created a showbag for each employee, filled to the brim with products and services from local businesses.

I took 20 people at a time with me to the new site on the train. We left the old building and walked to the train station together. I showed them how easy it was to swipe on and swipe off on public transport. During the entire journey I told them to pay attention, as at the end there'd be a quiz with an amazing prize.

When we arrived at the sparkling new building everything was ready and waiting for them. They were welcomed by local business owners; the IT team and building manager took them on a tour; and we played a scavenger hunt where the clues were little-known facts about the transformation.

They loved it. When they returned to the old office they were so excited and the news spread like wildfire.

> THINK OF DIGITAL TRANSFORMATION LESS AS A TECHNOLOGY PROJECT TO BE FINISHED THAN A STATE OF PERPETUAL AGILITY, ALWAYS READY TO EVOLVE FOR WHATEVER CUSTOMER WANTS NEXT, AND YOU'LL BE POINTED DOWN THE RIGHT PATH.
>
> AMIT ZAVERY

Don't get me wrong – there were still naysayers. But they were no longer loud and proud, and their numbers dwindled rapidly.

Play your cards right

The principle of play demonstrates that even the biggest luddites will be enticed to move to the bleeding edge of tech if we give them the right environment. Tribulation turns into transformation when curiosity is stoked.

In chapter 6 I talked about how AR was used in the PNG-based gold mining company I worked with. The local workers were curious about the AR world that we had created for autoclave training. The headsets were a toy with which they could explore another world.

I'm often brought into senior leadership teams with the objective of improving clarity, engagement and ownership of a grand transformational vision. As part of the process, I like to ask leadership team members which five emotions they think are critical to success, then dive deeper into the top five emotions they want the workforce to feel.

News flash: 99.9 per cent of people (including me, by the way – let alone senior leaders in large global organisations) do not talk about feelings comfortably. They get their backs up, shuffle their feet and avoid eye contact. It isn't fun.

I've since gamified the process. I use a deck of cards, each with one emotion printed on it, as a way to make the discussion about touchy-feely stuff feel less intimidating. People point to the cards, or pick up the cards they're referring to. It seems less personal and more playful this way.

> **AS ANY PARENT OF YOUNG CHILDREN CAN TELL YOU, TURNING AN ACTIVITY INTO A GAME IS A GREAT WAY TO GET PEOPLE TO PARTICIPATE IN IMPORTANT TASKS.**

As any parent of young children can tell you, turning an activity into a game is a great way to get people to participate in important tasks. An example of this could be parents attaching rewards to well-performed chores.

This strategy is best used when we need to motivate someone to perform an action. Gamification is an effective behaviour-change tactic that must be brought into large-scale tech transformations if we want to reduce the fear of the new and unknown, or simply gain widespread adoption of and compliance around new digitised processes.

Let's take a look at some gamification examples.

Gamifying Googlers' travel expense submissions

The challenge: Google needed to motivate its employees to submit their travel expense information on a regular schedule.

Gamified solution: When Google employees take a work trip, they receive an allowance for each location. Google gamified the expense process by letting employees who didn't spend their entire allowance choose what happened to the remaining money – they could be paid out in their next paycheque, save the funds towards a future trip or donate it to a charity of their choice. The rewards were time-bound and expired if employees didn't stick to the submission schedule.

Results: Gamifying Google's travel expense system translated into 100 per cent compliance within six months of the program launch.

Microsoft staffers weigh in on language localisation

The challenge: Microsoft has myriad language localisation needs for its many products, and ensuring that translations were accurate and made sense was a huge task for just one team.

Gamified solution: Microsoft built a 'Language Quality' game, involving a very simple Silverlight application that let users view screens to check for language accuracy. Microsoft included intentionally poor translations to ensure its employees were actually paying attention.

Results: The Language Quality game encouraged 4500 users to review 500,000 screens to correct or improve translations of their native languages. Microsoft Japan took a company-wide day off to play the game and ended up winning the leaderboard.

Cisco employees play their way to social media mastery

Challenge: Cisco had invested in a global social media training program for its employees and contractors. But with over 46 courses in the program, it was overwhelming to figure out where to start.

Gamified solution: Cisco introduced three levels of certification for the social media training program – Specialist, Strategist and Master – as well as four sub-certification levels for the HR, external communications, sales and internal partner teams. It also mixed in team challenges to incorporate a healthy dose of competition and collaboration into earning social media certifications.

Results: Since gamifying its training program, more than 650 Cisco employees have been certified and more than 13,000 courses taken.

Strategies used to engage mobile gamers, such as badges and rewards, are now finding their way into non-gaming activities such as education, fitness, banking and more. Self-care app Headspace is a brilliant example of this. Human psychology cultivated effectively through an experience can yield promising results. Headspace taps into the things that drive and motivate users to take action. As part of their profile in the app, users get to see a dashboard of statistics with attention given to the

> **PLAY IS FUNDAMENTALLY IMPORTANT FOR LEARNING 21ST CENTURY SKILLS, SUCH AS PROBLEM SOLVING, COLLABORATION, AND CREATIVITY.**
>
> AMERICAN ACADEMY OF PEDIATRICS

current streak. The gamification techniques found in this type of interface and data help turn an activity into a habit.

Sometimes simply having a visual reminder of potential loss can be enough to get users to continue their streaks. This is a perfect example of loss aversion. The thought of losing something such as a streak (hello, Snapchat?) can be just as strong a motivator as gaining something.

I've found this is true in encouraging behaviour change in large organisations. Leaderboards, points and streaks applied to change management efforts are more effective when the potential loss is emphasised.

Get your creative juices flowing and apply these ideas to your digital transformation, too.

THE CREATION OF SOMETHING NEW IS NOT ACCOMPLISHED BY THE INTELLECT BUT BY THE PLAY INSTINCT.

CARL JUNG

Incorporating play into the workplace

Play has an image problem. Some organisations regard play as frivolous – a waste of time, a distraction or a pointless exercise. Play is usually described as a break from 'real work.'

But it's not. You see, the opposite of play isn't work, it's disengagement. Partaking in play actually improves work quality.

Research has found play at work is linked with less fatigue, boredom, stress and burnout in individual workers. Play is also positively associated with job satisfaction, a sense of competence, and creativity. Studies show that when a participant receives a task that is presented playfully, they are more involved and spend more time on the task.[38]

The benefits of play for work teams include increased trust, bonding and solidarity, and a decreased sense of hierarchy. The entire organisation is better off: play evokes a friendlier work atmosphere, increases employee commitment to work, promotes more flexible organisation-wide decision-making and increases organisational creativity.

Play expert Dr Stuart Brown outlines the eight play personalities:[39]

1. **The Joker:** As the name suggests, these people are the clowns. They're fun, silly and nonsensical. This play personality is most prominent in young children. Skits, improv and charades fall under this personality.

2. **The Kinesthete:** This is about physical activity with no emphasis on winning over someone or dominating a competition. Think dancing, Pilates, skipping and slacklining.

3. **The Explorer:** This is about exploring physical, mental, emotional or spiritual realms. I have a bit of the explorer in me. Each year I travel to new countries and am regularly seeking out new restaurants, day trip routes, plays and people.

4. **The Competitor:** This is where coming in first is everything. Most gamers (physical board games or video games) have this play personality, and it's the most common catered to in organisations.

5. **The Director:** This play personality likes to orchestrate something – whether it's a trip, party or office workshop.

6. **The Collector:** This personality is about collecting anything you could think of: clothes, vintage memorabilia, photographs or Star Wars dolls.

7. **The Artist/Creator:** This is about artistic work using the hands – whether it's fashion illustration, clay sculpture or writing a DJ anthem using technology.

8. **The Storyteller:** This play personality focuses on 'once upon a time' and loves to use their imagination to create other worlds and universes. Activities in this personality may include writing prose, reading fiction books and watching fantasy movies.

After reading the list, you can see most people – and organisations – tend to focus on a subsection of these play types. To be more inclusive and spread the play mindset further, we must consider other play personalities and weave them into practice.

To do this, first make a list of what your organisation currently provides in terms of play at work. Do you have a range of options to suit all the play personalities? Or does your organisation only cater to the Competitor play personality with your ping-pong table?

Find out what types of play activities employees gravitate to. If you're a small organisation, you can ask what kind of things people like to do for fun. For a larger organisation, an online survey can help you get some ideas. From there, you can begin to identify which play personalities are not being covered.

Co-create activities with your people to cover all the play personalities. Get people involved! Crowdsource ideas and let people have some skin in the

CO-CREATE ACTIVITIES WITH YOUR PEOPLE TO COVER ALL THE PLAY PERSONALITIES.

game. Implement the ideas that make sense, and watch participation – and your organisation's capacity for creativity and problem-solving – spread like wildfire.

PAUSE AND REFLECT

- How can you incorporate playfulness and a sense of curiosity into the transformation process?

- In what ways can you encourage experimentation and risk-taking within the organisation? Reflect on strategies to create a safe space for trying new approaches, allowing for failure as a learning opportunity, and promoting a culture that celebrates curiosity, exploration and outside-the-box thinking.

- How can you personally model and promote a playful mindset? Reflect on how your leadership shadow (your own behaviour, attitudes and communication style) might influence people's perception of playfulness and its role in transformation. Consider how you can encourage others to embrace a playful mindset by leading by example, sharing success stories that highlight the benefits of play, and creating opportunities for collective play and team-building activities.

CHAPTER 13

THE PRODUCTION PRINCIPLE

Production involves taking action, delivering results and combining everything needed for the transformation in a cohesive and integrated way. It means setting clear goals and objectives, enlisting the right resources at the right time, and executing your plan with precision and focus. It also means being accountable for results and continually measuring and evaluating progress to ensure the organisation is on track to meet its goals.

Expert orchestration of talent, teams and technology is what separates Michelin from mediocre. It takes a lot of effort to create a seamless dining experience that leaves customers feeling so happy they talk about the experience fondly for years to come. Everyone – from the head chef to the sous chef, maître d', sommelier, host and more – is aligned and headed in the same direction. The same holds true for any organisation trying to achieve success in today's competitive world. It's not just about hiring top talent; it's about bringing them together and unlocking their potential as a high-performing team.

IN THE GLOBAL WAR FOR TALENT, HAVING PEOPLE WITH THE RIGHT CHARACTER AND CAPABILITY MAKES A WORLD OF DIFFERENCE TO HOW FUTURE FIT AN ORGANISATION IS.

In the global war for talent, having people with the right character and capability makes a world of difference to how future fit an organisation is. If the people at the top are all cut from the same cloth nothing will change. The right people can make the impossible possible. Change won't happen unless leaders realise that what got them to where they are today won't get them to where they need to be tomorrow.

Having 'A' players is one thing; unlocking their potential as an all-star team is another. Sometimes it's about transforming 'B' and 'C' players into an 'A' team. Have you watched *The Mighty Ducks*? A classic coming-of-age movie in the 90s, it underscored the importance of working as a team. The character Gordon Bombay says:

> *Have you guys ever seen a flock of ducks flying in perfect formation? It's beautiful. Pretty awesome the way they all stick together. Ducks never say die. Ever seen a duck fight? No way. Why? Because the other animals are afraid. They know that if they mess with one duck, they gotta deal with the whole flock. I'm proud to be a Duck, and I'd be proud to fly with any one of you. So how about it? Who's a Duck?*

Each person in the group is important, but when working together they become more powerful than the sum of their parts.

So how do we create a team of people who can work together effectively to achieve organisational goals? The first step is to hire people with diverse skills, abilities and backgrounds. The second step is to create a culture that values teamwork, collaboration and communication. This means breaking down silos, encouraging cross-functional

146

collaboration and recognising and rewarding team success over individual achievements.

One way to do this is through team-building exercises and activities that promote trust, communication and cooperation. These can include anything from outdoor adventures to escape rooms to cooking classes. The key is to create an environment and make space for team members to get to know each other on a personal level.

Another way to promote teamwork is through using technology. With the rise of remote work, organisations need to use technology to facilitate collaboration and communication among team members. Make it the norm to have cameras turned on during team calls. Technology can help teams stay connected, share information and work together regardless of their location.

However, technology alone is not enough. Organisations also need to create a culture that supports innovation and experimentation. This means giving team members the freedom to try new things, fail, and learn from their mistakes. It also means creating a safe space to share their ideas and opinions without fear of judgement or retribution.

Creating a high-performing team is not easy, but it's not impossible. It requires hiring the right people, creating a culture that values teamwork and collaboration, and using technology to facilitate communication and cooperation. By doing these things, organisations can

IN TODAY'S ERA OF VOLATILITY, THERE IS NO OTHER WAY BUT TO RE-INVENT. THE ONLY SUSTAINABLE ADVANTAGE YOU CAN HAVE OVER OTHERS IS AGILITY, THAT'S IT. BECAUSE NOTHING ELSE IS SUSTAINABLE, EVERYTHING ELSE YOU CREATE, SOMEBODY ELSE WILL REPLICATE.

JEFF BEZOS

unlock the potential of their employees and create an all-star team that can achieve great things together.

Make no mistake, it really is like putting together a star-studded production.

Taking cues from the Phantom

I saw *The Phantom of the Opera* at the Sydney Opera House. I had incredible seats and could see into the orchestra pit and glimpse the back of the stage.

It was a seamless production. This does not happen by accident. I can only imagine the brutal work that goes into the efficient coordination of props, costumes, actors, dancers, music and lighting.

It looked effortless; but just like a change transformation, several elements needed to merge and complement rather than repel each other to make it work:

- The producer – akin to the architect of the transformation vision; usually the CEO of the organisation.

- The lead actor – the person leading the transformation effort; the 'face' of the change. For a large-scale ERP implementation this is usually the CIO; for a shift in branding or customer strategy this is usually the CMO.

- The supporting cast – the people on the ground who make change happen. They are project managers, change champions, business process leads, solutions architects, data migration consultants and so forth.

THE FUTURE FIT ORGANISATION

- The orchestra conductor – the person leading the music that makes the production sizzle and adds that extra bit of oomph. The 'music' in a transformation is change management, training and communication. It makes a play go from meh to magnificent, and is remembered for years to come.

- The orchestra itself – the often-hidden heroes in a transformation: change management experts, e-learning developers, communications professionals, content creators and so forth. When they're doing their job well you shouldn't be able to discern them; it just all flows together.

Productions, like transformations, come together because each 'actor' knows their role, there are countless rehearsals to create a shared understanding of other people's roles and lines, and the more you 'rehearse' (come together, meet, workshop, co-create, collaborate, develop rapport), the more polished the production.

Prism, play and production

All three principles – prism, play and production – must coexist to achieve future fitness (see figure 13.1).

What happens when one is missing? Let's take a look:

- **Prism + production = arduous conquest:** This state is where it's all serious with no fun. Any progress towards change feels hard. It's all head, no heart. There is no laughter in the hallways and no jokes or emojis in Slack channels.

Figure 13.1: Prism, play and production

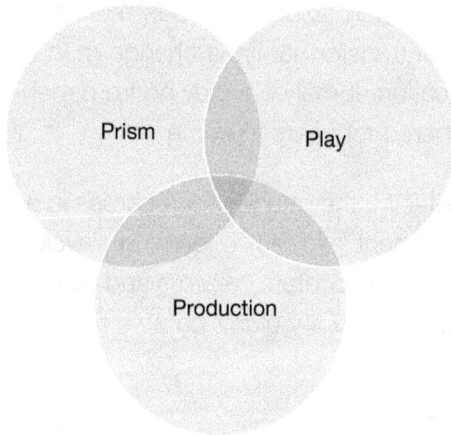

- **Prism + play = engaged chaos:** The business won't be running for much longer, certainly not profitably, if all everyone does is mess around. Goals aren't set, never mind met! No-one is held accountable and the organisation will atrophy. There's a lot of heart, but no head. The organisation lacks logic, planning and analytical ability.

- **Play + production = organised contempt:** There is significant wasted effort with rework and redesign the norm, rather than the exception. A lack of empathy, understanding and acceptance results in the wrong problem being solved, solutions being created that miss the mark. There is some head and a good pair of hands to move the organisation towards its transformational goals, but not much heart.

Now, if you have all three? Winner winner.

By applying the three principles of prism, play and production, organisations can build the agility, resilience and adaptability needed to thrive in today's fast-paced and ever-changing business landscape.

They understand the needs, constraints, challenges and wants of stakeholders – whether they are end users, clients, customers or other business units. They build healthy doses of curiosity and light-heartedness into their transformation. They ensure there is a solid production team to lead the organisation in the right direction, with the right people, at the right time and in the right manner. It's not enough to rely on past successes – to truly achieve future fitness, organisations must be willing to embrace change, take risks and continuously evolve and innovate.

The truth about digital transformation

Okay, here it is: the truth about digital transformation is that it's not about digital. It's not about fortifying the tech stack.

Organisations that are building future fitness are doing things differently. They identify what is no longer serving them, whether it be inefficient processes, out-of-date policies, misaligned values or irrelevant strategies.

ORGANISATIONS THAT ARE BUILDING FUTURE FITNESS ARE DOING THINGS DIFFERENTLY.

Then they do something about it. They change. They get rid of what is no longer serving them, and replace it with something fit for purpose that will help them get to where they want to go and be who they want to be.

Money pouring in doesn't necessarily mean a significant paradigm shift is around the corner, as everything from 3D TVs to Amazon's delivery drones can attest. The history of tech is littered with the skeletons of failed investments. Here are a few examples:

- Google Glass was a wearable device with an optical head-mounted display that allowed users to access information hands free. The product was launched in 2013, but it was discontinued in 2015 due to poor sales and criticism over privacy concerns.

- Microsoft Kin was a smartphone targeted at young adults that was released in 2010. The product was discontinued after just 48 days on the market due to poor sales.

- Amazon Fire Phone was a smartphone released in 2014. The product was a commercial failure and was discontinued after just one year due to poor sales and negative reviews.

- Quibi was a short-form mobile video platform that launched in 2020. The service failed to gain traction and was shut down after just six months.

> **DON'T BE FOOLED BY SOME OF THE DIGITAL TRANSFORMATION BUZZ OUT THERE. DIGITAL TRANSFORMATION IS A BUSINESS DISCIPLINE OR COMPANY PHILOSOPHY, NOT A PROJECT.**
>
> **KATHERINE KOSTEREVA**

Notice something in common? In each of these cases, the entire production was built without people's wants and needs as its guiding north star.

These examples highlight the importance of understanding peoples' needs and wants rather than blindly investing in technology. Without a clear understanding of what the market wants, even the most innovative technology can fail.[40] 'If you build it they will come' only works in the movies and, newsflash, you're not Kevin Costner.

A more accurate line might be: 'If you co-create it, they will come.' Involve your people in the change you want to make in the business. You see, humans are hardwired to value and endorse what they create. I've seen this play out countless times where I have suggested to my clients that they involve people earlier, and let them have a voice more often. Buy-in and support for the change accelerates.

I was invited to a 'Drive and Dine' event with Ferrari where this principle played out. Ferrari has a high-tech in-showroom customisation studio where you can literally create the car of your dreams from scratch – from the colour of the leather stitching to the wheels to the strength of the speakers in the sound system.

Guess what the rate of Ferrari ownership is after visitors complete this experience? An impressive 98 per cent plus. It's proof that us humans subconsciously support what we create with our own two hands.

So create opportunities for people to get some skin in the game. If you ask the right questions, you'll be surprised at the answers you get back. Chances are, you'll create an even better solution than the one you had been mulling about in your head.

To become future fit, organisations must identify what is no longer serving them and implement changes that align with their vision, values and the impact they want to make in this world. The most important part is that they must not neglect the human element. Inviting employees to co-create solutions and participate in the transformation process

TO BECOME FUTURE FIT, ORGANISATIONS MUST IDENTIFY WHAT IS NO LONGER SERVING THEM AND IMPLEMENT CHANGES THAT ALIGN WITH THEIR VISION, VALUES AND THE IMPACT THEY WANT TO MAKE IN THIS WORLD.

ensures that the change is meaningful, accepted and sustainable. The future belongs to organisations that recognise the importance of involving their people in their transformation efforts.

PAUSE AND REFLECT

- How can you ensure you have the right cast of individuals involved in the transformation journey? Have you got an experienced director (change management expert) who will put together your production? Reflect on the diversity of skills, expertise and perspectives needed to drive successful transformation. Consider how you can identify and engage key stakeholders, assemble a high-performing team and foster collaboration and synergy among team members.

- How can you effectively coordinate the roles and responsibilities of each cast member in your transformation? Reflect on the importance of clear role definitions, effective delegation and transparent communication to ensure that everyone understands their part and contributes to the transformation's success.

- How can you support and empower your cast members during the transformation journey? Reflect on strategies to provide the necessary resources, training and support to enable individual and collective growth. Consider how you can cultivate a positive and inclusive culture, celebrate achievements and provide coaching and feedback to help cast members excel in their roles.

CHAPTER 14

FUSING FUTURE FITNESS TOGETHER

So what does a future fit organisation do that others don't? Let's revisit some key insights from this book. The only thing that hasn't changed is the failure rate of change (70 to 80 per cent depending on the piece of research you read). As Alvin Toffler said, the illiterate of the future – and, I'd argue, the illiterate of today – will be those who cannot learn, relearn and unlearn. It has nothing to do with reading or writing. Modern advancements are only possible if we unlearn behaviour that is no longer serving us, and learn how to behave in new ways that support performance and growth.

Nearly 84 per cent of digital transformations do not achieve their objectives.[41] Leaders often seek to solve problems by adding more technology to their stack, but contemporary and mature organisations realise the tool is only powerful if people use it to its full potential.

Recall the previous chapters where I introduced the principles of prism, play and production. This is what it looks like in practice when it's done well:

- **Prism:** Organisations doing this well understand that diversity is key to success. They actively seek out diverse perspectives, experiences and backgrounds in their employees, customers and partners. They recognise that a diverse workforce leads to more innovation and better decision-making, and they create an inclusive culture that allows everyone to bring their full selves to work.

- **Play:** Organisations doing this well understand that experimentation, creativity and play are essential to innovation. They create an environment where employees feel safe to take risks and try new things, and they encourage a culture of learning and growth. They recognise that playfulness and creativity can lead to breakthrough ideas and new ways of doing things.

- **Production:** Organisations doing this well understand that execution and delivery are just as important as innovation and creativity. They have strong processes and systems in place that allow them to consistently deliver high-quality products and services. They focus on operational excellence and are regularly looking for ways to improve their processes and workflows.

Future fit organisations are diverse, inclusive, creative and invest in execution. They recognise that success requires a balance of innovation and delivery, and they are constantly striving to improve in both areas.

We can conclude that future fit organisations are those who are doing the following three things very well: the people stack, organisational readiness and learning and unlearning. Let's look at each of these in summary.

Power up your people stack

As I write this, Elon Musk is making headlines for firing nearly half of X's (formerly known as Twitter) workforce – about 3,700 jobs – just over a week after becoming the platform's owner.[42] In Indonesia, the GoTo Group, an IPO formed by unicorns Gojek and Tokopedia, also announced mass layoffs: about 1,300 jobs.[43] And it's not just the big guys. Australian startup Mr Yum reduced its headcount by 17 per cent in August 2022, followed by 40 more staff in March 2023.[44] Many other organisations have followed suit. I spoke to partners in the Big Four consulting firms who admitted the market was 'softening' and that anyone on the bench was reshuffled domestically to in-flight projects.

In some situations, headcount reduction – removing blocks from your people stack – is logical and necessary. But in many cases, doing so means missed opportunities to strategically reverse-Jenga the people stack – that is, build it, don't dismantle it!

In Twitter's case, staff were rehired just days after being fired. But was there sufficient analysis undertaken to confirm the organisation was rehiring people with the right attitude and the right experience? Who knows.

The future fit organisation undertakes strategic workforce planning: thinking ahead and projecting the character and capability mix required six months, a year and a few years from today.

It's also a case of making the most of the talent you have in your people stack. Anything AI related seems to attract investment so easily from venture capitalists and the private equity world. What everyone seems to gloss over is that

THE REALITY IS, WORKERS HAVE TO CONTINUOUSLY UPSKILL – FOR ORGANISATIONS TO STAND STILL FINANCIALLY.

these investments will not realise their desired outcomes if people don't readily accept and adopt the changes technology will bring. It is nonsensical to invest so much in tools without paying equal if not more attention to the people who will ultimately be using them.

The reality is, workers have to continuously upskill – for organisations to stand still financially. Not investing in upskilling will mean regression financially.

While digital solutions often empower employees to make better decisions, they also cause upheaval as highly manual tasks are automated. We shouldn't fear this – it's an amazing opportunity to expand job roles, redefine talent sources and revolutionise how we reskill and retrain. The future fit organisation will require rapid learning of technology and tools, where the knowledge worker and value-enriching tasks become the norm. Advancements that are cutting edge today may not exist in five years' time, and this necessitates building flexibility and agility into our capital and human resource plans.

SUCCESS IS NOT JUST ABOUT HAVING THE RIGHT PEOPLE WITH THE RIGHT SKILLS, BUT THE RIGHT MIX OF PEOPLE BOTH IN WORKFORCE AND DELIVERY TEAMS.

Success is not just about having the right people with the right skills, but the right mix of people both in workforce and delivery teams.

We need a new breed of worker – an intoxicating hybrid blending the very best of social skills (influence, persuasion, EQ and teaching others) with processing ability (active listening, critical thinking, reasoning and comprehension) and cognitive prowess (creativity and mathematical reasoning). It is about balance. STEM skills are important, sure, but they are insufficient in isolation.

In the not-too-distant future, qualities such as curiosity, empathy and sincerity will be sought after because these are key to nurturing an innovative mindset and an open culture. In our increasingly hyperconnected world, it is only the ability to authentically connect with people that will cut through the noise and inspire change.

> **IT IS ONLY THE ABILITY TO AUTHENTICALLY CONNECT WITH PEOPLE THAT WILL CUT THROUGH THE NOISE AND INSPIRE CHANGE.**

We must start hiring and developing people based on character or attitude, rather than simply skills or experience. As Dame Minouche Shafik, President of Columbia University, said, 'In the past jobs were about muscles, now they're about brains, but in future they'll be about the heart.'

Here are some of the benefits of character-based hiring:

- **Flexibility and adaptability:** When you hire for character, you prioritise qualities such as a growth mindset and a willingness to learn. These traits enable employees to quickly adapt to changing circumstances and acquire new skills as needed, which is valuable in dynamic environments.

- **Cultural fit:** Hiring individuals with the right character and values helps to build a cohesive organisational culture. When employees align with the company's values, they are more likely to work well with others, collaborate effectively and exhibit discretionary effort.

- **Long-term potential:** By focusing on character, you identify candidates with the potential to grow and develop within the organisation. While skills can be taught and developed over time, character traits such as integrity, resilience and a positive attitude are near impossible to instill if they don't already exist.

- **Building capability:** Hiring for character allows you to prioritise potential and invest in employee development. When you bring in individuals with the right attitude and aptitude, you can provide them with training, mentorship and growth opportunities to build the specific skills and capabilities needed for their roles. This approach fosters a learning culture and allows employees to reach their full potential.

- **Employee engagement and retention:** Hiring based on character contributes to higher levels of employee engagement and job satisfaction. When employees feel valued for their character traits, they are more likely to be motivated, committed and loyal. This reduces turnover and helps retain top talent.

Character-based hiring allows organisations to prioritise qualities that lead to long-term success, and cultivate a positive work culture. This is challenging when recruitment is a chaotic and reactive process.

> **IT IS NOT THE STRONGEST OF THE SPECIES THAT SURVIVES, NOR THE MOST INTELLIGENT. IT IS THE ONE MOST ADAPTABLE TO CHANGE.**
>
> **CHARLES DARWIN**

Too many businesses are in feast-or-famine mode: win a project; secure a big customer account; get shortlisted on a tender, madly scramble and corral whoever has a pulse within the organisation and recruit the rest in a frenzy. Or close a site; finish a project; lose a big customer; start getting rid of people left, right and centre. And then the madness starts again.

Don't do it. Get off the hamster wheel. The people stack is what will see you through good times and bad relatively unscathed.

Make sure you're stacking yours up with the right stuff.

Focus on readying

I've made a living thanks to the natural human response to resist change. If humans had evolved to be more accepting and embracing of the new and foreign, I'd be below the breadline!

It is essential to understand how best to support people to get ready for a change. The future fit organisation has the maturity to realise resistance isn't a bad thing. In fact, it's just a thing that happens. Instead of fighting it, ignoring it or delegating it, they proactively manage it. They put on their green hat and red hat. Heard of this indirect problem-solving approach?

Edward de Bono was a Maltese physician, psychologist and philosopher. De Bono originated the term 'lateral thinking', a method of hacking problems in creative and surprising ways, and created the Six Thinking Hats approach in the mid 1980s.

The green hat is the creative hat. You explore a range of ideas and possible ways forward using this hat. The red hat, 'the hat for the heart', represents feelings and instincts. When you're engaged in this type of thinking, feelings are expressed without having to justify them logically.

The future fit organisation uses the green hat to creatively and proactively support people to be 'change ready', shortening the emotionally rocky phases of denial, anger and scepticism. We need to use unconventional approaches if we are to move people quickly into experimentation and acceptance of change.

Putting a red hat on means deeply thinking about how people are feeling about a change, and what feelings we wish to

PEOPLE DON'T RESIST CHANGE. THEY RESIST BEING CHANGED.

PETER SENGE

evoke to enable readiness for a change. This is a productive and healthy lens to look out from when we are making plans for change.

So how exactly do you enable organisational readiness? Here are some best-practice change management strategies that help ready people for change:

- **Communication and transparency:** Effective, *early* and *frequent* (emphasis on the latter two, which are key) communication builds trust and ensures employees are aware of the changes taking place. It is important to be transparent about the rationale for the change and how it will impact the organisation and employees early. Clear and consistent messaging reduces resistance to change.

- **Training and development:** Providing employees with the necessary skills and knowledge to adapt to new technology is crucial. This can be accomplished via training sessions, workshops and e-learning modules. In some cases, organisations may need to hire new staff with specific skill sets to help drive the transformation forward.

- **Strong leadership:** Effective leadership is crucial for successful change. Leaders need to be visible, accessible and supportive throughout the transformation process. They must also be able to communicate the vision and objectives of the change and inspire employees to embrace the new way of working.

- **Pilots and testing:** Testing and piloting new technology can help to identify any issues before a full-scale implementation. This approach can also help to build momentum and gain buy-in from employees who will see the benefits of the new technology first-hand.

162

- **Agile methodology:** Agile methodologies are increasingly being used to manage change in organisations. This approach involves breaking down complex projects into smaller, manageable pieces and iterating quickly based on feedback. This allows you to adapt to changing circumstances and identify issues early.

There are several examples of organisations that have successfully implemented digital transformation by ensuring their people were ready for change. One is McDonald's, which underwent a significant digital transformation in recent years. The company recognised the need to adapt to changing customer preferences and improve operational efficiency. To achieve this, McDonald's invested in self-order kiosks, mobile ordering and delivery services. Extensive training was provided to ensure employee comfort with the new technology.

Another example is Microsoft, which shifted its focus from traditional software licensing to cloud-based services. The company provided extensive support for customers who were transitioning to the cloud and made sure their own people understood the impact of this strategy pivot. Microsoft also used a pilot approach, testing new technology with a small group of customers before rolling it out to the wider market.

An investment of time and effort is required to ensure an organisation is ready for change. By using effective change management strategies and techniques, you can prepare employees, reduce resistance and build momentum towards a successful transformation.

Invest in continuous learning and unlearning

Learning and unlearning are crucial components of personal and organisational growth. As the world continues to evolve rapidly, it is essential to adapt and acquire new skills to remain relevant. Future fit organisations recognise this fact and are investing in their employees' learning and development to stay ahead of the curve.

Do you remember when you first travelled to a foreign country? I recall my first time travelling to Japan as a teenager. I learned basic phrases in Japanese to order food, ask for directions or enquire about a product or service. I unlearned the knee-jerk reaction of greeting people in the way that is common in the West – to shake their hand while maintaining eye contact. I relearned how to greet people as per Japanese custom: a deep bow with eyes cast downward.

> WITH FAST IDEAS COMES FASTER INNOVATION: 60 PER CENT OF APPLE'S REVENUE COMES FROM PRODUCTS THAT DIDN'T EXIST FOUR YEARS AGO. THAT'S A BLISTERING PACE OF INNOVATION. EXPECT THAT TO BECOME THE NORM IN MOST INDUSTRIES AS THE FUTURE ACCELERATES, PRODUCT LIFECYCLES COLLAPSE, AND DISRUPTION DISRUPTS.
>
> JIM CARROLL

Here's another thought: where did you learn how to drive? I learned in Australia where cars are right-hand drive, cities have many roundabouts and give-way signs and you stay in the left lane, except when you are wanting to overtake.

I then moved to Los Angeles on scholarship during my undergraduate degree. It took intense concentration and focus to learn how to drive on the right-hand side of the road, and I had to unlearn the tendency to give way to the vehicle on my right at a four-way intersection sans traffic lights. There are no roundabouts in California. I had to relearn the rules of the road in a new country.

How can you ensure the learning and unlearning muscles don't atrophy in your organisation?

One best-practice strategy is to conduct regular skills assessments to identify skill gaps and development areas. You can then create customised training and development programs that address these areas. For example, Airbnb created a program called Airbnb Academy to help its hosts learn skills such as hospitality, communication and business management to improve guest experiences.

Another effective – but challenging – strategy is to create a culture of continuous learning and development. Cultures takes time to build, and it takes even more effort to change. This involves encouraging and rewarding employees for seeking out new knowledge and skills, as well as providing resources and opportunities for them to do so. As I mentioned earlier, Google offers employees 20 per cent of their work time to pursue personal projects and interests that align with the company's goals.

Organisations can use change management techniques to facilitate learning, relearning, and unlearning. This involves identifying and managing resistance to change, communicating the benefits of learning and development, and providing support and resources throughout the process to embed the desired new behaviours.

ORGANISATIONS CAN USE CHANGE MANAGEMENT TECHNIQUES TO FACILITATE LEARNING, RELEARNING, AND UNLEARNING.

> **CHANGE IS THE LAW OF LIFE AND THOSE WHO ONLY LOOK TO THE PAST OR PRESENT ARE CERTAIN TO MISS THE FUTURE.**
>
> **JOHN F KENNEDY**

Learning and unlearning are critical for personal and organisational growth, particularly in a rapidly changing world. Future fit organisations play an active role in their people's continuous learning. They place a stake in the ground. They explicitly assess which behaviours and skills are no longer serving them. They identify newer, more efficient and productive behaviours and skills. Most importantly, they dig into their pockets and put their money where their mouths are. They help their people to learn these new behaviours and skills, and unlearn the old ones.

By conducting regular skills assessments, creating a culture of continuous learning and utilising change management techniques, organisations can enable readiness to change and ensure their employees have the skills and knowledge needed to succeed.

Ultimately, there are three main characteristics of the future fit organisation. They are the ones that reverse-Jenga their people stack, focus on readying instead of resisting and invest in helping their people learn and unlearn.

I'm sure Alvin Toffler would agree.

PAUSE AND REFLECT

- Are you actively seeking out and embracing new ideas, technologies and trends that have the potential to shape the future of your industry or organisation? Reflect on your openness to change, curiosity and willingness to explore new possibilities that may challenge the status quo. Have you leveraged and integrated technology to enhance organisational efficiency, productivity and customer experiences? Reflect on your adoption of digital tools and technologies, and how they are aligned with the organisation's strategic goals.

- How are you fostering a culture of continuous learning? Are you walking the talk? When have you learned something new? Reflect on your commitment to personal growth and how you encourage others to expand their skills and knowledge. Consider how you create opportunities for experimentation, innovation and professional development to stay ahead in an ever-evolving business landscape.

- Have you understood the impact of macro-environmental trends to your organisation, and are you doing something about them? Have you resourced and budgeted for change management support accordingly?

CHAPTER 15

ORGANISATIONS DON'T CHANGE, PEOPLE DO

It would be remiss of me to end this book without highlighting a common scenario I've encountered over my decade of change and transformation experience: leaders expect everyone to change, except themselves.

Throughout the years I have seen some exceptional leaders who were able to influence workforces of up to 200,000 to do things differently to the way they've been done in the past. I have also experienced cold and disconnected leaders who couldn't influence an Eskimo towards a log fire.

Observing the above-average leaders I've noticed a common theme: they all exhibit the ABC qualities and execute the ABC activities as pictured in figure 15.1.

If the leadership activities are the bones, the tendons that hold them together are the qualities that leaders exhibit during a change effort.

Figure 15.1: The ABC qualities and activities[45]

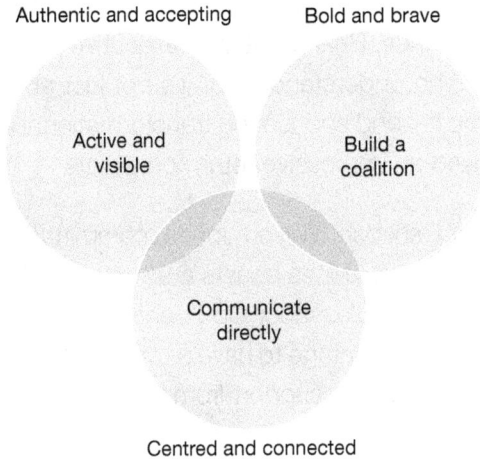

Authentic and accepting   Bold and brave

Active and
visible

Build a
coalition

Communicate
directly

Centred and connected

Prosci, one of the early movers and shakers in change management training and certification, states that executive sponsors of transformational change do three things:

1. Be active and visible

2. Build a coalition

3. Communicate directly.[46]

Have you heard the saying 'It's not what you say, it's how you say it?' It's the same with leadership roles and activities. It's not what you do but *how* you do it. A leader's sponsorship of change is the most important contributor to change management success.[47]

I suggest leaders at all levels in the organisation must have the ABC qualities when engaging with employees about change, disruption and innovation.

Leaders who have executed the three activities with equal parts head and heart will achieve great outcomes for their organisations such as a spike in key metrics. Brian Fontaine, executive vice president of Bose, is a leader who understands that it's not just about what you do, but how you do it – and sponsoring transformational change is no different. He enjoyed an impressive return on assets.

The former CEO of Oshkosh, Wilson Jones, committed to becoming a people-first organisation. Jones boasts a 93 per cent CEO approval rating on Glassdoor, with Glassdoor Co-Founder and CEO stating, 'It can be a real recruiting advantage to have a top-rated CEO at the helm of a company who has strong support from his or her employees.'

The best CEOs are inspiring, trustworthy, innovative and can be great motivators for people to bring their best selves to work.' These are CEO traits that can inspire a movement, drive energy and enthusiasm and unlock discretionary effort. And you only have to look at the glowing Glassdoor reviews of Microsoft CEO Satya Nadella to see that he is known for exhibiting those ABC qualities. In Nadella's book, *Hit Refresh*, he states the 'C' in 'CEO' stands for 'culture'.[48] He understands the criticality of culture and its ownership by leaders at the top of the organisation.

Authentic and accepting; active and visible

The most evolved leaders regard being authentic and accepting as bumpers on a bowling lane – the two qualities gently guide their active and visible sponsorship in the right direction, avoiding the dreaded gutter balls!

Leaders must be seen – and seen in the right way – during change.

It's not enough to say you support the change. Leaders must be seen to actively participate in the change in an authentic and accepting way. This encourages others to be part of the change, reducing resistance and scepticism.

IT'S NOT ENOUGH TO SAY YOU SUPPORT THE CHANGE.

During times of disruption and turbulence, followers need to feel the leader is transparent in all communications within the work environment.[49] Leadership expert Peter Northouse says, 'Followers and leaders are inextricably bound together in the transformation process. Authentic transformational leadership is socialised leadership, which is concerned with the collective good.'[50]

Real and transformative leadership has a positive effect on how followers see themselves. It helps them make better decisions and take positive actions that progress the common good. Authentic leaders genuinely care about the mission, inspire a common vision, and provide clear guidance for the team to follow.

Leaders whose words and actions don't align will be viewed as inauthentic, undermining any support for the change and tarnishing their reputation.

There's nothing worse for employee morale, change adoption and company reputation than leaders who practise the 'Do as I say, not as I do' mantra. When this occurs, you can almost see the loss of enthusiasm and goodwill, and the embedding of scepticism and betrayal in their people's eyes. It's like watching the air go out of a balloon – with cynicism and disappointment taking its place.

> **AS I GROW OLDER, I PAY LESS ATTENTION TO WHAT MEN SAY. I JUST WATCH WHAT THEY DO.**
>
> ANDREW CARNEGIE

Think of the executive who demands cost cutting, laying off thousands of people while giving himself a $10 million bonus; the manager who says she believes in work-life balance then calls her team at all hours of the night; the leaders who say they believe in and value their people, then proceed to reject every request for additional training or conference attendance; the supervisor who criticises everyone for taking a bit longer for lunch on Fridays, but accepts invitations for client golf days.

Remember the backlash against former disgraced British prime minister Boris Johnson when he was caught sans mask, not social distancing, and even organising booze-fuelled parties at Downing Street during the peak of London's lockdown period?

Many culture change efforts deteriorate into oblivion because the entire C-suite isn't seen to be engaging with or supporting the change. People are looking to their leaders for signals on what they should be focusing on. When leaders are absent from the change, people (often subconsciously) think the change isn't important and they shouldn't spend any energy on it.

Bold and brave; build a coalition

Building a coalition is like establishing the foundations of a house. You need its support to hold the walls up. Leaders must be bold and brave to build a coalition of support.

Building a diverse coalition of supporters for the change at all levels of the organisation is necessary to gain sufficient momentum to disrupt the status quo. It requires leaders to boldly and bravely back an initiative that has a very real (and high) chance of failure.

A coalition is a powerful, enthusiastic, diverse team of volunteers from across an organisation who put new strategies into effect and support the transformation effort. Coalitions can be seen in the political arena; President Obama's winning coalition in 2012 was a diverse cross-section of the community, running the gamut of age, race, religion and ideology.

Dr John Kotter, one of the grandfathers of change, states the most important aspect of a guiding coalition is its diversity.[51] An effective coalition team is comprised of individuals from across the organisation who bring unique skills, experiences, perspectives and networks to the table. Their distinct views allow the team to see all sides of an issue and enable the most innovative ideas to emerge; their varied roles and titles give credibility to the change effort; and their enthusiasm helps push the campaign forward with the speed and momentum necessary for success.

Centred and connected; communicate directly

Starting off on a transformation journey without communicating it is like organising an Oscars-worthy gala and not sending invites out.

Communication heals most wounds, but when it's ineffective and disconnected, wounds are more like viruses and very problematic to cure.

Leaders must be connected to the change vision and communicate this directly with employees. They must wholeheartedly believe the change is central to the organisation's success, and stand firm in their conviction when pushed and prodded for deeper answers or explanations about its rationale and impacts. People want to follow and look up to their leaders. Leaders must communicate and connect with the vision for change to increase buy-in, adoption and commitment to the future state.

Holmes research indicates the cost of poor communication is US$37 billion for just 400 US and UK companies alone.[52] This is not surprising. Bad communication leads to bad decisions, misunderstandings and a general disintegration of effective working relationships.

It's a leader's job to articulate a common vision, objective and set of values that resonate with the whole team. NASA astronaut Scott Kelly was once encouraged by fellow astronaut Cady Coleman to be more transparent and keep the public in the know at all times, so he made a point of sharing his stories and experiences. His leadership communication style helped build public interest and support for NASA's work.[53]

Indra Nooyi, former chairman and CEO of PepsiCo, said, 'The one thing I've learned is: don't lie to the people. Don't tell your people one thing when the reality is something different.'[54] Her unflinching (and sometimes unpopular) forthrightness was a huge factor in Nooyi's success. Over the long term, she proved her detractors wrong as PepsiCo's revenue increased from US$35 billion in 2006 to US$63.5 billion in 2017, with shareholders seeing a 162 per cent return.

Say what you mean, be true to your word and follow your conscience. Nooyi's fearless communication style shows that being honest to a fault may not be a fault at all.

I had a boss who was more comfortable communicating via email than in person. She rarely engaged in person at the office; she would only attend the occasional (not even once a quarter) lunch. She was so removed from the requirements of the business that it became obvious she felt vulnerable and insecure. She wasn't confident and felt her authority would be undermined if her insights and contributions didn't add immediate value to the issues at hand. Her poor communication skills were eventually exposed when, during a strategy meeting, a member of the board entered the room and started to ask pointed questions.

I felt a responsibility to have my boss's back. I took the initiative to address the questions – only to be interrupted by the board member who specifically wanted a response from my boss. The outcome was inevitable and soon she was out the door.

The point of engagement

At this point, you may be thinking, 'Wow, that's a lot of work. I can't afford to spend more time on these change leadership activities. I have a day job to do.'

I say this to all my clients: you can either spend a reasonable amount of time proactively engaging with people, or an unreasonable amount of time putting out fires and battling resistance. It's your choice.

Consider these statistics. Employee engagement – or, rather, a lack thereof – is a big problem for organisations around the world. According to data collected by Gartner in 2Q22, employees showing high discretionary effort – willingness to go above and beyond at work – dropped from 17 per cent in 1Q22 to 15 per cent.[55] We can argue this suggests people are less engaged in their work.

So, what happens to an employee's engagement when they're affected by a large-scale transformation? For some people, transformational change represents excitement, opportunity and a fresh start; most, though, experience change as a time of fear, despair and uncertainty. (Given the 50-plus transformations I've worked on, trust me when I tell you that most fall into the latter bucket.)

Here are some warning signs and a practical set of questions that may indicate your approach to employee engagement isn't working:

- **Visible observed indicators:** Look at how people are showing up to work every day. Are they engaged in meetings (heck, do they even attend them?) and one-on-one conversations? Are they displaying the same discretionary effort as they were prior to the change?

- **Health and wellness data:** Are you seeing a spike in sick days and absenteeism? What about 'present absenteeism' – where people are physically at their desks but mentally and psychologically checked out? Are people less social and active in the workplace? Do people choose to forgo proper lunch breaks because they are too busy? Is it seen as a badge of honour that people are taking on multiple roles, either 'double hatting' or 'triple hatting'?

- **Evidence of change fatigue:** Are people praying the change 'will all blow over soon', or 'will stop when the next CEO arrives'? Do people look and sound exhausted and harried? Does the phrase 'head down, bum up' get bandied about? Do people avoid truly connecting with others? Do people seem numb when new changes are announced?

Engagement drops during large transformations because most change is not managed well, and little to no attention is paid to people's mental and emotional states.

> **ENGAGEMENT DROPS DURING LARGE TRANSFORMATIONS BECAUSE MOST CHANGE IS NOT MANAGED WELL, AND LITTLE TO NO ATTENTION IS PAID TO PEOPLE'S MENTAL AND EMOTIONAL STATES.**

Why should you care? 'Show me the money!' I hear you say. Well, digest this: Forbes says the cost of disengagement is 34 per cent of an employee's annual salary.[56] That's $3400 for every $10,000 they make. The median salary in Australia hovers around the AU$80,000 mark.[57] This means one person's disengagement is costing you AU$27,200 a year, in the form of higher absenteeism, lower productivity and lower profitability. For a 1000-employee business that's AU$27.2 million per annum.

I have seen far too many disengaged employees intentionally slow down work, take multiple aimless laps around the office and generally waste time and airspace on the company's dime. Don't let this happen in your organisation.

PAUSE AND REFLECT

- How well do you understand your role as a leader in sponsoring and championing change within your organisation? Who's done it well? Who's done it not so well? Where do you think you fall along this continuum? What needs to change?

- Have you identified and communicated a compelling vision that inspires and motivates your team to embrace transformation? How do you know? What can you do differently to improve the 'stickiness' of your message?

- Are you actively fostering a culture of engagement and participation, allowing employees to have a voice and contribute to decision-making processes about transformational changes? Have you considered the risks and costs of disengagement, such as decreased productivity, increased turnover and missed opportunities for innovation? What can be done to mitigate these risks?

FINAL
THOUGHTS

Becoming a future fit organisation requires a deep commitment to change and transformation. It's not about adding more technology to the stack or ticking boxes for diversity and inclusion. It's about understanding the power of the human spirit, the full spectrum of emotions and the catalysing role organisational culture has in driving digital transformation success.

We must recognise that change is difficult and resistance is an expected and completely normal response to anything new. It's important to build relational intelligence and encourage healthy and constructive expressions of all emotions. By doing so, you can shorten resistance cycles and move towards becoming a more agile and adaptable organisation.

Leaders must be willing to take risks, reframe failure as feedback and learn from mistakes. They must be champions of change, living and breathing this ethos and leveraging their gravitas to encourage peer support for the change. They must recognise the value of diverse perspectives in creating a holistic approach to the adoption and integration of new technologies.

FUTURE FIT ORGANISATIONS MUST PRIORITISE SYSTEMISATION, CONSISTENCY AND STANDARDISATION TO ACHIEVE EXCELLENCE IN SERVICE, QUALITY AND EXPERIENCE.

Future fit organisations must prioritise systemisation, consistency and standardisation to achieve excellence in service, quality and experience. This not only saves costs, but reduces waste, minimises glitches and strengthens client and employee satisfaction.

The three principles of prism, play and production must form the foundation of all transformation programs. They set the stage for an organisation's entire workforce to embrace change, approach the foreign with curiosity and understand their role in making change happen.

Becoming a future fit organisation requires a holistic approach that values people, emotions, culture and diversity. It's about setting a new standard that normalises agility, innovation and adaptability to better respond to the ever-changing business landscape. Newer technologies such as social media and mobility have made the world more transparent, accessible and accountable – in the past, our organisation's culture evolved with the technology. However, for the next leap of technological progress, we need to simultaneously work on the cultural leap as well.

By doing so we can transform our future flab into the future fit.

ABOUT
THE
AUTHOR

Friska Wirya is the powerhouse behind Fresh By Friska – a change management consulting, coaching, facilitation and training service for executives, teams and global businesses.

A top 50 change management thought leader, sought-after TEDx speaker and multiple-award-winning consultant, Friska has led change efforts in six of the seven continents, and is most known for her work with large corporates – including a US$170 million cost saving for the biggest gold miner in the southern hemisphere, executing the digital response to COVID for Australia's number 1 university, and partnering with a large engineering company to win the race to net zero.

Friska's differentiation is symbolised in her business name – it's about a fresh take. This means doing away with the old ways that are no longer serving us, and being open to exploring and experimenting with the new and foreign – whether it be culture, technology, structure or strategy. Friska helps achieve that elusive behaviour change within organisations.

When she is not engaged with clients, she can be found satisfying her wanderlust, leading masterclasses on executive presence and expanding her Pilates repertoire.

Visit freshbyfriska.com to subscribe to The Change Cohort and get early previews, special offers and information on new products. You can also find Friska on Instagram and LinkedIn.

ACKNOWLEDGEMENTS

Writing this book has been an extraordinary journey fuelled by my unwavering passion for change and its immense potential to shape – and improve – our future. From the very beginning, my intention was clear: to equip businesses and individuals with the mindset and methods necessary to navigate the turbulent waters of change and emerge stronger and more resilient than ever before.

I firmly believe that change has the power to either cripple us or propel us forward, as an individual or business – and it is in our hands to determine which path we choose. It is this conviction, coupled with my deep-rooted desire to see organisations thrive and individuals flourish, that inspired me to embark on this writing odyssey.

There is immense transformative power in the change management discipline. I have witnessed first-hand the immense challenges organisational leaders face when confronted with change, and I have witnessed the incredible triumphs made possible when change is embraced with an open mind, a courageous heart and a robust change management strategy.

Change is not a passing trend; it is the next normal. In today's fast-paced and ever-evolving world, businesses of all sizes and industries must develop their change management muscles if they wish to stay competitive, innovative and relevant. This book is my humble contribution to this critical conversation, offering insights, strategies and practical guidance to help build your change management capabilities and navigate the complex landscape of transformation.

I am deeply grateful for the opportunity to share my knowledge, experiences and hard-earned lessons through the pages of this book. My hope is that it will serve as a guiding light for leaders, change agents and individuals seeking to embrace change, harness its potential and pave the way for a future that is not only prosperous but also deeply fulfilling.

A special mention goes to Stu, who has been my sounding board/confidant/brainstormer and avid provider of comic relief. Your willingness to engage in spirited debates and share your diverse perspectives has broadened my horizons and elevated the quality of this work.

I extend my heartfelt appreciation to the readers, whose curiosity and open minds have motivated me to delve deeper into the subject matter and craft a book that resonates with their aspirations. Your enthusiasm and eagerness to embrace change inspire me to continue sharing my ideas and insights with the world.

Thank you to all of you who have joined me on this transformative journey. Together, let us build a world where change is no longer feared but embraced as a catalyst for growth, innovation and personal evolution.

Remember: no change, no progress.

REFERENCES

1   R Dobbs, J Manyika and J Woetzel, *No Ordinary Disruption: The Four Global Forces Breaking All the Trends*, PublicAffairs, 2015.

2   Innosight, *2021 Corporate Longevity Forecast*, May 2021, accessed 30 June 2023.

3   M Baker, 'Gartner HR Survey Reveals 88% of Organisations Have Encouraged or Required Employees to Work From Home Due to Coronavirus', Gartner, 19 March 2020, accessed 13 June 2023. gartner.com/en/newsroom/press-releases/2020-03-19-gartner-hr-survey-reveals-88--of-organisations-have-e

4   PwC, *Tech breakthroughs megatrend: how to prepare for its impact*, 2016, accessed 30 June 2023. pwc.com/gr/en/publications/assets/tech-breakthroughs-megatrend-how-to-prepare-for-its-impact.pdf

5   Accenture, 'Global Venture Capital Investment in Fintech Industry Set Record in 2017, Driven by Surge in India, US and UK, Accenture Analysis Finds', 28 February 2018. https://newsroom.accenture.com/news/global-venture-capital-investment-in-fintech-industry-set-record-in-2017-driven-by-surge-in-india-us-and-uk-accenture-analysis-finds.htm

6   B Ewenstein, W Smith and A Sologar, 'Changing change management',
    McKinsey & Company, 1 July 2015, accessed 30 June 2023. mckinsey.
    com/featured-insights/leadership/changing-change-management;   V
    Marcelino, 'Digital Transformation Success and Failure – Part I Insights
    from Industry and Grey Literature', EINST4INE, 14 June 2022, accessed
    30 June 2023. https://www.einst4ine.eu/digital-transformation-success-
    and-failure-part-i-insights-from-industry-and-grey-literature/

7   Owl Labs, *State of Remote Work 2021*, accessed 30 June 2023. https://
    owllabs.com/state-of-remote-work/2021/

8   S Janiak, 'Fueling Organizational Growth Through Digital Fluency',
    Forbes, 20 September 2022, accessed 30 June 2023. https://www.
    forbes.com/sites/deloitte/2022/09/20/fueling-organizational-growth-
    through-digital-fluency/?sh=7ba07da178e5

9   C Block, '12 Reasons Your Digital Transformation Will Fail', *Forbes*,
    16 March 2022, accessed 4 July 2023. https://www.forbes.com/
    sites/forbescoachescouncil/2022/03/16/12-reasons-your-digital-
    transformation-will-fail/?sh=6adf7d641f1e

10 N Nohria and M Beer, 'Cracking the Code of Change', *Harvard Business
    Review*, May–June 2000, accessed 14 June 2023. hbr.org/2000/05/
    cracking-the-code-of-change; RS Kaplan and DP Norton, 'The Officer
    of Strategy Management', *Harvard Business Review*, October 2005,
    accessed 30 June 2023. https://hbr.org/2005/10/the-office-of-strategy-
    management

11 S Antliff, 'Workplace overwhelm: how to protect your team from change
    fatigue', *Atlassian*, 28 June 2021, accessed 4 July 2023. atlassian.com/
    blog/leadership/change-fatigue

12 American Psychological Association, 'Stress and decision-making
    during the pandemic', 26 October 2021, accessed 15 June 2023. apa.
    org/news/press/releases/stress/2021/october-decision-making

13 Ibid.

14 J Thomson, 'Company Culture Soars At Southwest Airlines', *Forbes*,
    18 December 2018, accessed 30 June 2023. https://www.forbes.com/

sites/jeffthomson/2018/12/18/company-culture-soars-at-southwest-airlines/?sh=9c2392c615f2

15 J Simpson, 'Finding Brand Success In The Digital World', *Forbes*, 25 August 2017, accessed 15 June 2023. forbes.com/sites/forbesagencycouncil/2017/08/25/finding-brand-success-in-the-digital-world/?sh=7bb54bcd626e

16 Jungle, 'How Many Tweets Does It Take To Trend?', 23 November, accessed 20 June 2023. https://jungle.marketing/news/how-many-tweets-does-it-take-to-trend/

17 A Hayes, 'The Human Attention Span', *Wyzowl*, 31 May 2023, accessed 15 June 2023. wyzowl.com/human-attention-span

18 D Zheng, 'The 15 Second Rule: 3 Reasons Why Users Leave a Website', *The Daily Egg*, 14 May 2020, accessed 4 July 2023. crazyegg.com/blog/why-users-leave-a-website

19 G Harrison and M Lucassen, 'Stress and anxiety in the digital age: the dark side of technology', *OpenLearn*, 1 March 2019, accessed 30 June 2023. https://www.open.edu/openlearn/health-sports-psychology/mental-health/stress-and-anxiety-the-digital-age-the-dark-side-technology

20 McKinsey & Company, 'Unlocking success in digital transformations', 29 October 2018, accessed 4 July 2023. mckinsey.com/capabilities/people-and-organizational-performance/our-insights/unlocking-success-in-digital-transformations

21 Australian Human Rights Commission, '2010 Workers with Mental Illness: a Practical Guide for Managers', n.d., accessed 4 July 2023. humanrights.gov.au/our-work/1-mental-health-workplace

22 Medibank, *The Cost of Workplace Stress in Australia*, August 2008, accessed 4 July 2023. medibank.com.au/content/dam/client/documents/pdfs/The-Cost-of-Workplace-Stress.pdf

23 *Workhuman*, 'SHRM/Globoforce Survey Reveals Human-Centered Approaches in the Workplace Help Organizations Better Recruit

and Retain Employees', 24 January 2018, accessed 15 June 2023. workhuman.com/press-releases/globoforce-shrm-human

24 A Mann and N Dvorak, 'Employee Recognition: Low Cost, High Impact', Gallup, 28 June 2016, accessed 30 June 2023. gallup.com/workplace/236441/employee-recognition-low-cost-high-impact.aspx

25 Gartner, 'Gartner HR Research Reveals 82% of Employees Report Working Environment Lacks Fairness', 8 November 2021, accessed 30 June 2023. gartner.com/en/newsroom/press-releases/2021-08-11-gartner-hr-research-reveals-eighty-two-percent-of-employees-report-working-environment-lacks-fairness

26 iGrad, 'The Cost of Replacing an Employee and the Role of Financial Wellness', *Enrich*, n.d., accessed 4 July 2023.

27 K Benson, 'The Magic Relationship Ratio, According to Science', The Gottman Institute, n.d., accessed 30 June 2023. gottman.com/blog/the-magic-relationship-ratio-according-science

28 Transparency Market Research, 'The Cost of Replacing an Employee and the Role of Financial Wellness', n.d., accessed 4 July 2023. transparencymarketresearch.com/extended-reality-xr-market.html

29 A Hargrove, JM Sommer and JJ Jones, 'Virtual reality and embodied experience induce similar levels of empathy change: Experimental evidence', *Computers in Human Behavior Reports*, August–December 2020, 2.

30 E Hopper, 'How Your Social Life Might Help You Live Longer', *Greater Good Magazine*, 28 July 2020, accessed 3 July 2023. greatergood.berkeley.edu/article/item/how_your_social_life_might_help_you_life_longer

31 J Holt-Lunstad, TB Smith and JB Layton, 'Social Relationships and Mortality Risk: A Meta-analytic Review', *PLOS Medicine*, 2010, 7(7).

32 KI Alcaraz et al., 'Social Isolation and Mortality in US Black and White Men and Women', *American Journal of Epidemiology*, 2019, 188(1): 102–109.

33 A Cimermanaite, 'The AR and VR market size is predicted to reach $451.5 billion by 2030', *Metaverse Post*, 27 December 2022, accessed 3 July 2023. mpost.io/the-ar-and-vr-market-size-is-predicted-to-reach-451-5-billion-by-2030

34 R Williams, 'Why Empathy is the Most Critical Leadership Skill', *Medium*, 16 January 2023, accessed 3 July 2023. medium.com/age-of-awareness/why-empathy-is-the-most-critical-leadership-skill-73e00d299089

35 Businessolver, *2019 State of Workplace Empathy Report*.

36 Pumble, 'Communication in the workplace statistics 2023', n.d., accessed 4 July 2023. pumble.com/learn/communication/communication-statistics

37 Grammarly, 'The State of Business Communication: New Threats and Opportunities', 21 February 2023, accessed 4 July 2023. grammarly.com/business/learn/state-of-business-communications-2023

38 Association for Psychological Science, 'Playing Up the Benefits of Play at Work', 13 October 2017, accessed 3 July 2023. psychologicalscience.org/news/minds-business/playing-up-the-benefits-of-play-at-work.html

39 T Pearce, 'Use the eight Play Personality Types to bring learning to life', Untold Play, n.d., accessed 3 July 2023. untoldplay.com/blogs/untold-play/use-the-eight-play-personality-types-to-bring-learning-to-life

40 The Verge, 'The 84 biggest flops, fails, and dead dreams of the decade in tech', 21 December 2019, accessed 25 June 2023. https://www.theverge.com/2019/12/20/21029499/decade-fails-flops-tech-science-culture-apple-google-data-kickstarter-2010-2019

41 C Block, op. cit.

42 K Conger, R Mac and M Isaac, 'Elon Musk Fires Twitter Employees Who Criticized Him', *The New York Times*, 15 November 2022, accessed 26 June 2023. https://www.nytimes.com/2022/11/15/technology/elon-musk-twitter-fired-criticism.html

43 Reuters, 'Indonesia's GoTo to cut 1,300 jobs to step up cost cutting', 19 November 2022, accessed 3 July 2023. reuters.com/technology/indonesias-goto-cuts-1300-workers-or-12-total-employees-2022-11-18/

44 David Adams, 'Another 40 staff to go at Mr Yum as Australian startup readjusts to market downturn', SmartCompany, 22 March 2023, accessed 3 July 2023. smartcompany.com.au/startupsmart/news/40-staff-layoff-mr-yum-market-downturn

45 Adapted from Prosci, Primary Sponsor's Role and Importance', n.d., accessed 7 July 2023. prosci.com/resources/articles/primary-sponsors-role-and-importance

46 Ibid.

47 A Horlick, 'The most important contributor to change management success', Navigo, 31 March 2014, accessed 26 June 2023. https://www.navigo.ca/blog/most-important-contributor-change-management-success

48 S Nadella, *Hit Refresh: The Quest to Rediscover Microsoft's Soul and Imagine a Better Future for Everyone*, 2017, Harper Business.

49 Julie Kiehne, 'Authentic Leadership During Times of Change', in M Ohs (ed) *Change: A Leader's Perspective: Leadership Education Graduate Student Voices on 21st Century Change*, Winona State University, 2017.

50 PG Northouse, *Leadership: theory and practice*, Sage, 2016.

51 Kotter International, 'Guiding Coalition: A Dream Team to Help You Implement Strategy Quickly', Forbes, 8 February 2012, accessed 3 July 2023. forbes.com/sites/johnkotter/2012/02/08/guiding-coalition-a-dream-team-to-help-you-implement-strategy-quickly/?sh=7b2de54eb294

52 PRovoke Media, 'The Cost Of Poor Communications', 16 July 2011, accessed 3 July 2023. provokemedia.com/latest/article/the-cost-of-poor-communications

53 JM Olejarz, 'Life's Work: An Interview with Scott Kelly', *Harvard Business Review*, November–December 2017, accessed 26 June 2023. https://hbr.org/2017/11/lifes-work-an-interview-with-scott-kelly

54 D Novak, 'Follow Indra Nooyi's example: Become a leader people are excited to follow', CNBC, 12 September 2018, accessed 26 June 2023. https://www.cnbc.com/2018/09/12/pepsico-indra-nooyi-be-a-leader-people-want-to-follow.html

55 Gartner, 'Gartner HR Survey Shows Active Job Searching Has Declined in Australia for the First Time in Three Quarters', 2 August 2022, accessed 4 July 2023. gartner.com/en/newsroom/press-releases/2022-08-02--gartner-hr-survey-shows-active-job-searching-has-dec

56 K Borysenko, 'How Much Are Your Disengaged Employees Costing You?', Forbes, 2 May 2019, accessed 3 July 2023. forbes.com/sites/karlynborysenko/2019/05/02/how-much-are-your-disengaged-employees-costing-you/?sh=37211b523437

57 J McDonald, 'Average Salary In Australia: A Guide', *Forbes*, 22 June 2023, accessed 26 June 2023. https://www.forbes.com/advisor/au/personal-finance/average-salary-in-australia

www.ingramcontent.com/pod-product-compliance
Lightning Source LLC
Chambersburg PA
CBHW061020220326
41597CB00016BB/1759